FRANK D. GILROY

Volume Two
15 One-Act Plays

SMITH AND KRAUS PUBLISHERS
Contemporary Playwrights / Anthologies

If you require prepublication information about upcoming Smith and Kraus books, you may receive our semiannual catalogue, free of charge, by sending your name and address to *Smith and Kraus Catalogue, 4 Lower Mill Road, North Stratford, NH 03590. Or call us at (800) 895-4331, fax (603) 922-3348, website www.SmithKraus.com.*

FRANK D. GILROY

Volume Two
15 One-Act Plays

CONTEMPORARY PLAYWRIGHTS
SERIES

SK
A Smith and Kraus Book

A Smith and Kraus Book
Published by Smith and Kraus, Inc.
177 Lyme Road, Hanover, NH 03755

First Edition: May 2000
10 9 8 7 6 5 4 3 2 1

The Library of Congress Cataloging-In-Publication Data

Gilroy, Frank Daniel, 1925–
[Plays. Selections]
Frank D. Gilroy. —1st ed.
p. cm. — (Contemporary playwrights series)
Contents: v.1. Collected full-length plays — v.2. 15 one-act plays.
ISBN 1-57525-267-8 (v.2)
I. Title. II. Series.

PS3513.I6437 A6 2000
812'.54—dc21   00-038781

CONTENTS

❧

…and again

INTRODUCTION

An interview with Frank D. Gilroy that would have taken place if someone had asked the right questions.

INTERVIEWER: What is the hallmark of a valid one-act play?

GILROY: It's exactly as long as it should be and if you try to expand it beyond that point, you ruin it.

INTERVIEWER: How would you define a one-act play vis-à-vis a full-length play?

GILROY: It's a jab as opposed to a knockout punch—a sprint compared to a marathon.

INTERVIEWER: Could you phrase that more artfully?

GILROY: The one-act play is to the full-length as the short story is to the novel—the etude to the symphony.

INTERVIEWER: Do you always know it's going to be a one-act play before you write it?

GILROY: There is no "always" when it comes to play writing except that the most proven and skilled practitioner knows that he or she is *always* one play away from being an amateur.

INTERVIEWER: In *general,* do you know it's a one-act idea as opposed to a full-length idea when you set sail?

GILROY: You damn well better.

INTERVIEWER: What about serendipity?

GILROY: What about it?

INTERVIEWER: Columbus set sail for India and discovered America.

GILROY: He had a wider latitude than playwrights enjoy.

INTERVIEWER: Are you suggesting there is a formula for plays that must be strictly adhered to?

GILROY: Positively.

INTERVIEWER: Would you care to share it with us?

GILROY: If I knew what it was, I'd be glad to.

INTERVIEWER: Does anyone know this formula?

GILROY: No.

INTERVIEWER: Then what makes you so sure there is one?

GILROY: Because all plays that work, regardless of length or genre, achieve the same magical effect, which suggests a common source.

INTERVIEWER: Are you getting metaphysical?

GILROY: Not intentionally.

INTERVIEWER: You mentioned a "magical effect." Would you care to elaborate?

GILROY: If you're in the audience on one of those rare nights when everything's working, you lose yourself as the miracle unfolds.

INTERVIEWER: Could you say that plainer—omitting such words as "miracle"?

GILROY: When a play's cooking, you forget everything else. When it isn't, your ass twitches.

INTERVIEWER: Giving the bad one-act play a significant advantage over the bad full-length by nature of its brevity?

GILROY: That's one of its virtues.

INTERVIEWER: Can you will a one-act play into existence or does it, like the full-length, require inspiration?

GILROY: Anything that works in the theater demands inspiration, but a one-act requires proportionately less.

INTERVIEWER: In that case, why don't we have more of them?

GILROY: We do. Witness the thousand submissions the Ensemble Studio Theatre receives each year for its Marathon. What's lacking are subsequent outlets because of economic viability.

INTERVIEWER: English translation?

GILROY: Unless the same actors are suitable for all the plays that comprise an evening, it's too costly.

INTERVIEWER: Most of the plays in this volume were first presented at EST. Did you write them with EST in mind?

GILROY: Definitely. To know there's a theater space available primes the pump. Witness that the most prolific playwrights of late (Terrence McNally, A.R. Gurney, Lanford Wilson et al.) are closely identified with particular theaters.

INTERVIEWER: *Gotcha!*

GILROY: How so?

INTERVIEWER: Earlier you said all plays, short and long, require inspiration. Now you're saying they can be willed.

GILROY: What I'm saying is that knowing there's a theater looking forward to your next play is a mighty stimulus. When I was president of the Dramatists Guild, I sought to implement this notion by marrying playwrights of proven talent to college and university theater facilities—those wonderful state-of-the-art spaces that put Broadway and Off-Broadway to shame.

INTERVIEWER: Marry in what way?

GILROY: I wanted the college or university to subsidize the playwright for a year during which he or she would have ready access to their apparatus. If they wanted the playwright to teach and it was mutually agreeable—fine. But the playwright's primary obligation was to his or her own work. In other words, teaching wasn't a prerequisite. If the playwright came up with something the school would have first call on initial production.

INTERVIEWER: How did it go over?

GILROY: It didn't.

INTERVIEWER: Any nibbles?

GILROY: Yes, but when the colleges realized that the playwright wouldn't necessarily arrive with a play in hand—that they would have to gamble the same way playwrights do—they lost interest.

INTERVIEWER: May I ask a few questions about the plays in this volume?

GILROY: No.

INTERVIEWER: Why not?

GILROY: Once they're written they have to speak for themselves.

FAR ROCKAWAY

INTRODUCTION

William Schuman, composer, former head of the Juilliard, and president of Lincoln Center, invited me to write a short play, which would be done as a play and then translated into a dance by the choreographer Anna Sokolow. And then into an opera by Mark Bucci.

It was performed on channel thirteen celebrating the anniversary of Lincoln Center.

Far Rockaway, the play, thirteen scenes in fourteen pages, owes something of its conciseness to my admiration of Woyzeck.

ORIGINAL PRODUCTION

Far Rockaway was first presented on National Educational Television under the auspices of the Lincoln Center in September, 1965, with the following cast in order of appearance:

Michael St. John	Michael Higgins
Mrs. St. John	Frances Sternhagen
The Neighbor	Kay Medford
His Employer	Milo Boulton
Dr. Walgreen	Kermit Murdock
Desk Sergeant	Moses Gunn
The Priest	John Heffernan
Mrs. Brown	Ann Wedgeworth
First Gravedigger	Tom Pedi
Second Gravedigger	Lou Gilbert

Directed by Ulu Grosbard; staged for television by Kirk Browning; settings by Ed Wittstein; produced by Jac Venza.

SCENE I

MICHAEL ST. JOHN: *(Reading the inscription on a plaque.)* "On January fifth, at eleven A.M., Michael St. John, while strolling the beach at Far Rockaway, did kill a fleeing murderer."

MRS. ST. JOHN: I still don't know what he was doing at Far Rockaway at eleven a.m. on a Monday.

MICHAEL ST. JOHN: *(From the plaque.)* "…is hereby awarded this plaque for valor in the public interest."

MRS. ST. JOHN: I was doing my nails when my neighbor burst in.

THE NEIGHBOR: Michael killed a murderer at Far Rockaway. It just came over the radio.

MRS. ST. JOHN: Don't be absurd.

THE NEIGHBOR: Michael St. John.

MRS. ST. JOHN: I know my husband.

THE NEIGHBOR: Thirty-eight. Civil engineer.

MRS. ST. JOHN: Wouldn't harm a fly.

THE NEIGHBOR: This address.

MRS. ST. JOHN: What would Michael be doing at Far Rockaway at eleven A.M. on a Monday?

THE NEIGHBOR: She's got a point.

SCENE II

MICHAEL ST. JOHN: Ate my usual breakfast that morning. Left the house at the usual time.

MRS. ST. JOHN: Pecked me on the cheek as usual.

MICHAEL ST. JOHN: My subway pulled into the station. The doors opened…

THE NEIGHBOR: *(Reading from a newspaper.)* "The next thing I knew," said Mr. St. John, "I was standing on the beach at Far Rockaway, gun in hand, this fellow dead at my feet."

MRS. ST. JOHN: Far Rockaway at eleven A.M. on a Monday? I don't understand.

MICHAEL ST. JOHN: Neither do I.

THE NEIGHBOR: *(From the newspaper.)* "Mr. St. John suffered a partial amnesia induced by the…continued on page forty-eight."

HIS EMPLOYER: I've always been a good judge of men, but St. John—Mike, that is—fooled me. Been with my firm twelve years. Honest, competent, decent—but you'd never take him for a hero. Yes, I was really fooled by St. John—Mike, that is.

THE NEIGHBOR: They'd been trying to have children for a long time. Had given up, in fact.

MRS. ST. JOHN: There was blood on his cuff...a strange odor about him.

THE NEIGHBOR: She conceived that night.

HIS EMPLOYER: Mind if I call you Mike?

MICHAEL ST. JOHN: The neighborhood kids stopped letting the air out of my tires.

THE NEIGHBOR: In a word—he prospered.

SCENE III

HIS EMPLOYER: Just between us, Mike, what's it like to kill a man?

MICHAEL ST. JOHN: Sad.

THE NEIGHBOR: Could Gary Cooper put it better?

HIS EMPLOYER: I made him Chief of Sales.

MICHAEL ST. JOHN: I began to have nightmares.

THE NEIGHBOR: Some people can't stand prosperity.

SCENE IV

MICHAEL ST. JOHN: Oh, my God.

THE NEIGHBOR: *(Reading from a newspaper.)* "Mr. St. John's amnesia is of a temporary nature," said Doctor P. H. Walgreen, psychiatrist. "In short..."

DR. WALGREEN: ...he'll remember everything that happened, someday.

MICHAEL ST. JOHN: *Oh, my God!*

DR. WALGREEN: What did I tell you?

SCENE V

MICHAEL ST. JOHN: I'm not a hero.

MRS. ST. JOHN: The neighbors are sure we'll have a boy.

MICHAEL ST. JOHN: I didn't have to shoot that fellow.

MRS. ST. JOHN: It's very active just now—feel.

MICHAEL ST. JOHN: He'd broken his ankle—was lying helpless on the beach.

MRS. ST. JOHN: How cold your hand is.

MICHAEL ST. JOHN: He reached up—gave me his gun.

MRS. ST. JOHN: What shall we call it if it's a boy?

MICHAEL ST. JOHN: Je-*sus!*

MRS. ST. JOHN: And if it's a girl?

MICHAEL ST. JOHN: I didn't *kill* him…I *murdered* him.

MRS. ST. JOHN: You haven't heard a word I said.

SCENE VI

MICHAEL ST. JOHN: I didn't have to shoot that fellow.

HIS EMPLOYER: Your tie is stained.

MICHAEL ST. JOHN: He'd broken his leg.

HIS EMPLOYER: You need a haircut.

MICHAEL ST. JOHN: Handed me his gun…

HIS EMPLOYER: And a shine…

MICHAEL ST. JOHN: *I murdered him.*

HIS EMPLOYER: Something wrong, Mike?

SCENE VII

MICHAEL ST. JOHN: I want to report a murder.

DESK SERGEANT: The same one you reported yesterday?

MICHAEL ST. JOHN: I didn't have to kill him.

DESK SERGEANT: We've been over that.

MICHAEL ST. JOHN: Arrest me.

DESK SERGEANT: The law is satisfied.

MICHAEL ST. JOHN: Arrest me!

DESK SERGEANT: There's no complaint.

MICHAEL ST. JOHN: There's a body.

DESK SERGEANT: It's been accounted for.

MICHAEL ST. JOHN: But—

DESK SERGEANT: —It's been accounted for!

SCENE VIII

DR. WALGREEN: To demand a penalty of yourself that society doesn't require is neurotic.

MICHAEL ST. JOHN: I like the sound of that.

DR. WALGREEN: We must find out who you killed that morning at Far Rockaway.

MICHAEL ST. JOHN: A fellow named Brown.

DR. WALGREEN: We must discover your victim's name.

MICHAEL ST. JOHN: William Brown—it was in the papers.

DR. WALGREEN: We must learn for whom those bullets were *really* intended.

MICHAEL ST. JOHN: William Brown!

DR. WALGREEN: Shall we begin?

(*Howard exits, slamming the door.*)

SCENE IX

MICHAEL ST. JOHN: I've killed a man.

THE PRIEST: The confidences of the confessional are inviolate.

MICHAEL ST. JOHN: Can it be forgiven?

THE PRIEST: If it's repented.

MICHAEL ST. JOHN: Would I be here if I wasn't sorry?

THE PRIEST: Given the chance, would you do it again?

MICHAEL ST. JOHN: I want to say no—but it sticks in my throat.

SCENE X

MICHAEL ST. JOHN: I killed your husband.

MRS. BROWN: Please come in.

MICHAEL ST. JOHN: He was lying on the beach.

MRS. BROWN: Do you know how many men he killed?

MICHAEL ST. JOHN: His leg was broken.

MRS. BROWN: He raped his sister when she was eight.

MICHAEL ST. JOHN: Handed me his gun.

MRS. BROWN: Beat the children, so that one is crippled.

MICHAEL ST. JOHN: Two bullets in his heart—one in his head.

MRS. BROWN: God bless you.

MICHAEL ST. JOHN: I *murdered* him.

MRS. BROWN: Will you stay for tea?

SCENE XI

MRS. ST. JOHN: I needed butter—was phoning Michael at the office to bring some home, when my neighbor came in.

THE NEIGHBOR: I just passed Michael running down the street.

MRS. ST. JOHN: *(On the phone.)* May I speak to Mr. St. John, please…?

THE NEIGHBOR: Where's the fire? I shouted.

MRS. ST. JOHN: *(Still on the phone.)* There must be some mistake…

THE NEIGHBOR: "Far Rockaway," he shouted back. "A terrible blaze."

MRS. ST. JOHN: *(Putting down the phone.)* They say Michael hasn't been at the office in a week.

THE NEIGHBOR: Did you hear anything about a fire at Far Rockaway?

SCENE XII

MICHAEL ST. JOHN: *(He shivers.)* The water's colder than it looked.

SCENE XIII

FIRST GRAVEDIGGER: I heard it was suicide.

SECOND GRAVEDIGGER: There was talk.

FIRST GRAVEDIGGER: How is he buried in church ground?

SECOND GRAVEDIGGER: They stretch a point for heroes.

> *(Blackout.)*

THE END

PRESENT TENSE

INTRODUCTION

Curt Dempster founded the Ensemble Studio Theatre in 1972 or thereabouts.

He asked me if I had any one-acts to launch the theater.

I gave him *Present Tense* and the three plays that follow.

We tried them in that condemned warehouse at fifty-second and eleventh where EST resides to this day—the building still condemned as far as I know.

The tryout so well received that we moved the quartet Off-Broadway.

The origins of *Present Tense* (the title play) are not clear to me—nor, I suspect, were they ever.

The Vietnam War was on. I came late to acceptance it was an ugly blunder. Guilt and confusion about that is surely part of it.

But why is it so opaquely written that Stanley Richards, who included it in his *Best Short Plays* series, summed it up as "a few consequential hours in a marriage that may or may not be faltering."

As I write, it occurs to me that retitling it *We Regret to Inform You* would do a lot for clarity and intention.

ORIGINAL PRODUCTION

Present Tense was presented by the Ensemble Studio Theatre in 1972. The play was directed by Curt Dempster with the following cast:

Father. . . . . Biff McGuire
Mother. . . . . , , Lois Smith

SCENE I

Time: Tonight. Place: A suburban living room. At rise: Lights out. A door bell rings three times, a beat, three more rings. Lights up. Father is peering surreptitiously through a window that commands a view of the front door. Mother is seated across the room. The doorbell rings again, repeating the same pattern as before.

MOTHER: What are you waiting for—let her in.

FATHER: No.

MOTHER: Why not?

FATHER: Keep your voice down.

MOTHER: Why not?

FATHER: She'll keep us up all night.

MOTHER: I thought you liked her.

FATHER: I do.

mother Then why—

FATHER: —She never knows when to leave and I have to get up early. *(The doorbell again.)*

MOTHER: That doesn't sound like her.

FATHER: It's her.

MOTHER: She always goes dah-de-dah-de-dah. Are you sure it's her.

FATHER: She's wearing that checkered coat.

MOTHER: In this weather? *(The doorbell again.)* That's *not* her usual ring…She never drops in at night without calling…Supposing it's an emergency?

FATHER: She's smiling.

(Mother rises. Her movement draws his attention.)

MOTHER: I have to let her in.

FATHER: You don't believe me. You don't believe it's her.

MOTHER: All night I'd be wondering what she wanted. I wouldn't be able to sleep.

FATHER: Who do you think would be ringing that bell that I would want to hide from you? A cop with a warrant for a hit-and-run accident? A girl with a baby that she claims I'm the father of?

MOTHER: *(Starting for the door.)* I just have to.

FATHER: Supposing it's *not* her? *(She stops—regards him.)* Suppose it's somebody else?

MOTHER: Are you trying to upset me?

FATHER: It would be the end of trust between us.

MOTHER: If you're trying to upset me, you're doing a find job.

FATHER: Of course I could always claim the light was bad, that I mistook her for someone else.

MOTHER: *(Abandoning the idea of going to the door.)* It's not worth the fuss…She's probably gone by now anyway…Besides I'll see her tomorrow…But what do I say: "We didn't open the door when you rang last but I'd like to know what you wanted"?

FATHER: Tell her we were making love and the moment was crucial.

MOTHER: At a quarter past seven. *(He goes to her—begins to fondle her.)*

FATHER: Tell her I got this sudden letch in the middle of Walter Cronkite.

MOTHER: So that's what you had in mind. I'm relieved. I really am. I was beginning to get worried.

FATHER: *(Unbuttoning her.)* Tell her I was taking you on the living room floor while she was ringing. She'll like that.

MOTHER: I haven't had my pill today. *(The doorbell sounds—three rings.)* That's not her ring.

FATHER: *(Increasingly ardent.)* On the living room floor while Murry Fromson was speaking from a small hamlet thirty miles north of Saigon. *(Three rings.)*

(The lights going down. Their love play spiraling.)

MOTHER: *(Voluptuously.)* She always goes *dah*-de-*dah*-de-*dah*…And that checkered coat in *this* weather…*(Three rings, a beat, three rings.)*

SCENE II

Time: An hour later. Lights ups. Father, dressed as before, is peeking out the window as before.

MOTHER'S VOICE: *(Offstage.)* You're sure you want coffee?

FATHER: Yes.

MOTHER'S VOICE: *(Offstage.)* You know how it keeps you awake and you said you wanted to be up early.

FATHER: I want coffee. *(He anticipates her entrance; turns from the window as Mother, in negligee and robe, bearing coffee cups on a tray, appears; stops; regards him curiously.)* Something wrong?

MOTHER: You're dressed.

FATHER: *(Regarding himself—surprised.)* How about that?

MOTHER: We're going to bed soon.

FATHER: I did it without thinking.

MOTHER: Shoes, socks—everything.

FATHER: It's like this, baby: I'm leaving you and I wanted to be ready for a quick getaway once the cat was out of the bag.

MOTHER: You *always* put on your pajamas afterwards.

FATHER: If it will make you feel better I'll change.

MOTHER: *(Handing him a cup.)* Here.

FATHER: *(Raising his cup in toast.)* Your health. *(They sip.)* No word from Billy today?

MOTHER: We had a letter yesterday. I'd feel better if I'd taken the pill.

FATHER: What's life without a risk?

MOTHER: Listen to who's talking: wouldn't talk to me for a week the last time I even suggested another child.

FATHER: If I was a gambling man I'd lay odds we scored tonight.

MOTHER: That's not funny.

FATHER: I predict a bouncing-baby-something nine months from tonight. Circle your calendar and remember you heard it here first.

MOTHER: *(Reading him with astonishment.)* You've changed your mind. You *want* it to happen. *(His failure to respond confirms it.)* Why?

FATHER: Fools give you reasons.

MOTHER: This is a joke—

FATHER: —*It's not a joke! (Smiles and raises his hand in a three-finger salute to take the fierce edge off.)* Scout's honor.

MOTHER: I'm overwhelmed.

FATHER: "I'm dubious." "How do you do, Mr. Dubious?"

MOTHER: What are you nervous about?

FATHER: A man forty-five is about to assume the responsibilities of father-hood and she says "What are you nervous about."

MOTHER: Don't count your chickens. I mean how do you know we're still able.

FATHER: *I* knocked up my secretary not too long ago.

MOTHER: Was she the one at the door with the baby? *(He regards her blankly.)* Before when the doorbell rang you said it might be a girl with a baby.

FATHER: Okay, let's settle it once and for all: Who do *you* think was at the door? Who do *you* think was ringing that bell?

MOTHER: I think it was who you said it was.

FATHER: Cross your heart?

MOTHER: Yes.

FATHER: Despite the checkered coat in this weather?

MOTHER: Yes.

FATHER: Then the subject's concluded, finished.

MOTHER: Settled

FATHER: Buried.

MOTHER: Interred.

FATHER: Kaputt.

MOTHER: Terminee.

(He sits; picks up a newspaper.)

MOTHER: …Except for one thing.

FATHER: Interesting item here about the Viet Cong slaughtering the entire population of a hamlet.

MOTHER: I wonder what she wanted.

FATHER: Women, children, everyone.

MOTHER: If I don't find out I'll never get to sleep.

FATHER: Eighty-seven bodies—most of them mutilated.

MOTHER: I'm going to phone.

FATHER: No.

MOTHER: Why not?

FATHER: She'd keep you talking for hours.

MOTHER: You can close the door—go to sleep.

FATHER: *(Suggestively.)* I've got other plans, my pretty.

MOTHER: I think your eyes are bigger than your stomach.

FATHER: *(Feeling her.)* The better to eat you with.

(She starts to respond, then breaks away.)

MOTHER: No! Not till I call her.

FATHER: *(Gesturing to the phone.)* Be my guest. *(He returns to his chair and the paper. Puzzled by his sudden capitulation she just stands there.)*

MOTHER: I'm relieved. I was beginning to think there was something wrong—some reason you didn't want me to speak to her. *(She waits for him to comment, but he doesn't.)* Maybe you're right. Maybe I shouldn't. She *does* go on.

FATHER: Call her. *(She goes to him, toys with his ear. He stops her.)* I insist.

MOTHER: That's not fair—getting a girl all steamed up—

FATHER: —*Call her.*

MOTHER:…All right. *(She goes to the phone; picks up the receiver.)* There's no dial tone. *(She clicks the cradle.)*

FATHER: Eighty-seven bodies. More than half of them women and children.

MOTHER: *There's no dial tone.*

FATHER: Try the operator.

MOTHER: There's *no* tone at all. It's dead.

FATHER: Dead?

MOTHER: Dead.

(He goes to the phone, takes the receiver, listens.)

FATHER: You're right. It's dead.

MOTHER: It was working after supper. I called my mother. *(He has returned to his chair and the paper.)* What'll we do?

FATHER: Wait till it's fixed.

MOTHER: We have to report to it.

FATHER: By the time we wake up it will be taken care of.

MOTHER: It has to be reported.

FATHER: They won't send anyone till morning.

MOTHER: *I want it reported.*

(He rises—starts out.)

MOTHER: Where are you going?

FATHER: Your wish is my command.

MOTHER: You'll go to one of the neighbors—use their phone.

FATHER: That's right. *(Donning a jacket.)* While I'm gone read that article about the eighty-seven people the Viet Cong killed—most of them women and children.

MOTHER: It's lucky you're dressed.

FATHER: If I'm not back by dawn I want you to forget me—build a new life for yourself. *(He brushes her chin with his fist and exits.)*

MOTHER: Don't go to the Larsens. She and I aren't speaking. *(We hear the outside door close. She tries the phone again. Dead. She hangs up, absently tugs on the cord. It gives. Surprised, she pulls the cord till its severed end appears from behind the sofa; regards it.)*

SCENE III

Time: A half hour later. Lights up. Father and mother sitting. He reads his paper. She regards the severed phone cord on her lap.

MOTHER: …Not till morning.

FATHER: Not till morning.

MOTHER: Is that a company policy?

FATHER: I have no idea.

MOTHER: If it is, it should be changed…We ought to complain.

FATHER: Take a letter.

MOTHER: Suppose there was an emergency—someone trying to reach us?

FATHER: Such as?

MOTHER: It could be anything.

FATHER: Name three.

MOTHER: How could it be working after supper when I called my mother and an hour later the cord is broken.

FATHER: I'll bite.

MOTHER: It's like someone yanked it from the wall.

FATHER: You're *sure* you called your mother?

MOTHER: Of course.

FATHER: What *makes* you so sure?

MOTHER: I always call her after supper.

FATHER: What was the substance of the conversation?

MOTHER: What *she* did. What *I* did. How's her bursitis. The usual thing.

FATHER: In other words, nothing was said that would distinguish tonight's alleged call from the many thousands that have preceded it.

MOTHER: "Alleged"?

FATHER: *(Rising.)* Your Honor, I respectfully submit that the plaintiff, victim, witness, defendant (call her what you will) did not phone her mother tonight.

MOTHER: *I did so.*

FATHER: I submit she honestly, underline honestly, believes she called her mother after supper because she *always* calls her mother after supper.

MOTHER: She bought a blender today.

FATHER: I submit the phone cord...*(Picks up the cord—displays it to the "jury.") this* phone cord—was accidentally ruptured during the day by person or persons unknown. Possibly the maid in trying to dust behind the sofa.

MOTHER: The maid's off today.

FATHER: She moved the sofa and voila.

MOTHER: *The maid's off today.*

FATHER: Another outburst like that and I'll clear the court.

MOTHER: How could I know about the blender if I didn't call her?

FATHER: *Accidentally ruptured by person or persons unknown.*

MOTHER: We talked for over ten minutes.

FATHER: Case dismissed.

MOTHER: She asked if we'd heard from Billy.

FATHER: *The case is closed! (She is startled by his vehemence. He tries to make light of it.)* You know what you should do now? *(She just looks at him.)*

You should go to the kitchen and come back carrying a step ladder. I ask where you're going and you say...*(He waits for her to say it. She doesn't.) What do you say?*

MOTHER: *(Rotely.)* I'm taking my case to a higher court.

FATHER: *(A la circus music)* Da-da-da-da-*dah*. Dah-dah-dah-*dah*.

MOTHER: The last time the phone was out of order you nearly went crazy till they fixed it.

FATHER: I hope it's a girl. How about you?

MOTHER: *(Regarding the severed cord.)* It's like somebody pulled it...

FATHER: A boy or a girl?

MOTHER: ...Yanked it out of the wall.

FATHER: *A boy or a girl? (She regards him.)* Do you want a boy or a girl?

MOTHER: I don't care as long it's healthy.

FATHER: I figure we *have* a boy—let's balance things.

MOTHER: By the time he or she is twenty, we'll be sixty.

FATHER: I even have a name picked out.

MOTHER: Means we'll be tied down again for most of the rest of our lives.

FATHER: What a jolt when I walk in that office and start handing out cigars.

MOTHER: And then there's Billy. *(This gains his attention.)* How's he going to feel having a brother or sister twenty years younger than *he* is?

FATHER: It's got nothing to do with Billy.

MOTHER: He might not like it.

FATHER: *It's got nothing to do with him! (Reasonably.)* It's *our* decision. It's what *we* want. It has nothing to do with anyone else. Not Billy. Not anyone.

MOTHER: I guess so.

FATHER: You don't sound very enthusiastic.

MOTHER: It's such a shock. I'd resigned myself that I was never going to have another child. Now all of a sudden—

FATHER: —*It's not all of a sudden.*...I've been thinking about it for quite a while—considering all the pros and cons, the pluses and minuses...*(He waits for her to chime in. She doesn't. He primes her.)* The pros and cons, the pluses and minuses...

MOTHER: The ups and downs.

FATHER: The ins and outs.

MOTHER: The twists and turns.

FATHER: I didn't want to say anything till I was sure.

MOTHER: But suppose, just suppose, we can't? I mean let's not get our hopes too high.

FATHER: *(With absolute certainty.)* We're going to have another child—one way or the other.

MOTHER: "The other"?

FATHER: It's a sin to have all we have and not share it.

MOTHER: Are you talking about adoption?

FATHER: We could handle two or three kids with no strain at all. Even four.

MOTHER: I'm stunned.

FATHER: The boys in Billy's room—the girls in the guestroom.

MOTHER: When the Petersons adopted a child you said they were crazy.

FATHER: In a pinch we can convert the den.

MOTHER: You said it was buying other people's trouble.

FATHER: You're confusing adoption with second-hand cars—but what's the difference. The important thing is I've seen the light.

MOTHER: What happens when Billy comes home?

FATHER: Maybe we'll adopt one of every race, color, and creed—start our own United Nations.

MOTHER: I really think Billy should be consulted.

FATHER: Wouldn't that give the neighborhood a jolt.

MOTHER: After all, it's *his* home as much as ours.

FATHER: Not any more.

MOTHER: You mean because he's grown up, because when he gets back he'll go away to college? Is that what you mean?… *Isn't that what you mean?*

FATHER: Yes.

MOTHER: What about holidays—vacations? He'll still come home for those.

FATHER: *(Regarding the newspaper.)* Did you read this article?

MOTHER: I think he should be consulted

FATHER: Most of them women and children.

MOTHER: I wouldn't want him to think he's being pushed out of the nest.

FATHER: It opens your eyes: makes you realized there's some justification for this war.

MOTHER: What am I getting so upset about? First we have to give nature a chance. Then there's miles of red tape. By the time we're eligible, Billy will *be* home. He'll be consulted automatically.

FATHER: Who knows—maybe it will be like that professor said on TV: Maybe history will judge it to be a war of vital necessity for the preservation of the free world.

MOTHER: *(Regarding the severed cord.)* For the life of me I can't imagine how this happened.

FATHER: I did it.

MOTHER: It would take a strong pull.

FATHER: I'm small but wiry.

MOTHER: *(Starting from the room.)* Beats me.

FATHER: Where are you going?

MOTHER: To bed.

FATHER: You can't.

MOTHER: Why not?...Well?

FATHER: We have to wait for the repairman.

MOTHER: You said they wouldn't fix it till morning.

FATHER: They said there was an outside chance they'd send someone tonight.

MOTHER: I'm not staying up all night for a repairman.

FATHER: They said if he wasn't here by eleven he wasn't coming.

MOTHER: *(She'll wait with him.)* What's on TV?

FATHER: I'm sick of TV.

MOTHER: It's TV or solitaire?

FATHER: Did I tell you what happened when I went out to report that the phone wasn't working?

MOTHER: I can hardly wait.

FATHER: I met a fire-breathing dragon.

MOTHER: There goes the neighborhood.

FATHER: "Bon soir," I said—he was wearing a beret. No reply. Just stood there puffing.

MOTHER: Hey did I tell you—I haven't had a cigarette in three days.

FATHER: "Sprechen zie Deutsch?" "Habla Español?" "Capisce Italiano?" No dice.

MOTHER: I'd rather watch television.

FATHER: I started to run. A light at the Bradleys. I knocked—actually I pounded. Ed came to the door—didn't open it but I recognized his voice. "Who is it?" he said. "It's me," I said. "What do you want?" he said. "My phone is out of order and there's a fire-breathing dragon on my tail." *(Falsetto.)* "The Pringles aren't home you all."

MOTHER: I never liked them.

FATHER: On to the Kelehers. Ralph came to the peephold. I told him about the phone and the dragon. He said—

MOTHER: —"Go home and sleep it off"?

FATHER: No.

MOTHER: "We already gave"?

FATHER: He said, "Where's that ladder you borrowed last fall?" I said, "Ralph, don't you understand? There's a dragon chasing me?" He said, "That's what they all say."

MOTHER: It takes a dragon to show who your friends are.

FATHER: Now I was panicky. I raced to the Willowbys.

MOTHER: Walter said, "I'm from Missouri."

FATHER: Cora came to the door.

MOTHER: *She* said, "I'm from Missouri."

FATHER: Right.

MOTHER: You showed her the dragon.

FATHER: I wanted to but it was taking a leak and you know how Cora is.

MOTHER: Perry Como has a special on.

FATHER: To make a long story short—

MOTHER: —with Phil Silvers and—

FATHER: —*To make a long story short. (He gets her attention.)* I had to go six blocks before I found someone who would let me in. Of course you can't really blame people with all the crime and violence.

MOTHER: Sometimes I wonder if Billy isn't safer in Vietnam.

FATHER: You took the words right out of my mouth.

MOTHER: Who finally let you in?

FATHER: The drugs. The riots, The way they drive.

MOTHER: *Who finally let you in?*

FATHER: The Bronsons.

MOTHER: The Bronsons are away.

FATHER: "You poor man," they said. "An out-of-order phone and a dragon."

MOTHER: *The Bronsons are out of town.*

FATHER: Actually it was the Frawleys.

MOTHER: Why did you say the Bronsons?

FATHER: Because the Bronsons are funnier than the Frawleys and the world needs laughter.

MOTHER: I never thought of the Bronsons as funny.

FATHER: Close your eyes…*Go on. (She closes her eyes.)* Picture the Bronsons! His bloodhound eyes. Her wattles. His ears. Her ass.

MOTHER: *(Eyes open.)* I'm sorry but it's not amusing. And I'm surprised at *you*—making fun of people's physical characteristics.

FATHER: My grandmother had a baby when she was forty-six.

MOTHER: It's too late for Perry Como—let's see what else is on.

FATHER: You want to know the kind of paradise we're assigning those people to if we pull out of Vietnam? Look at Hungary—Czechoslovakia. And how about the way they treat Jews.

MOTHER: *(Reading* TV Guide.*)* There's a Gable movie.

FATHER: Don't get me wrong: I hate that war as much as I ever did. All I'm saying is that maybe it's not so black and white as we thought—maybe there's more justification for it than we've realized.

MOTHER: "The Barefoot Contessa" with Ava Gardner.

FATHER: You might say "If you hated it so much why didn't you talk your son out of going?" My answer to that is that there are certain decisions a man has to make for himself.

MOTHER: *Hey there's a Charlie Chan on nine.*

FATHER: Which one?

MOTHER: "The Case of the Devil Ring."

FATHER: Is that where his number one son goes to fight in Vietnam and the mother blames Charlie because he talked about World War Two too much? Made it sound glamorous—attractive?

MOTHER: One morning after you'd left for work, Billy asked me why you talked about World War Two so much. He said he was bored to tears with all those stories. I told him it would hurt your feelings if you knew he felt that way. He said okay, to spare your feelings he'd pretend they were interesting.

FATHER: That's a relief. You've got no idea how guilty I've felt about that. I can't tell you what a relief that is.

MOTHER: Then why aren't you relieved?

FATHER: I am. I feel great.

MOTHER: What time did you they say that repairman would be here if he was coming?

FATHER: Eleven o'clock.

MOTHER: It's almost ten.

FATHER: If he'd come to me and said he didn't want to go to Vietnam I would have told him to do what his conscience dictated. But he never came to me—never expressed any objection to the war.

MOTHER: The Hubbard boy is going to school in Montreal.

FATHER: Is that a dig at me?

MOTHER: No.

FATHER: You think Hubbard told his kid "Burn your draft card. Go to Canada"?

MOTHER: You were talking about the war and I just happened to think of him.

FATHER: Hubbard's kid did it on his own. The parents were heartbroken.

MOTHER: They visited him at Christmas.

FATHER: He can never come back to this country without going to jail. The boy's life is ruined.

MOTHER: This country isn't the whole world and time works wonders.

FATHER: *The boy's life is ruined! (His ferocity rivets her.)* As Charlie Chan used to say, "You can't have your fortune cookie and eat it too." Or was that Davenport?

MOTHER: Davenport?

FATHER: Richard F. Davenport. Red hair, freckles, moustache.

MOTHER: Who's he?

FATHER: The dissection caper—nineteen sixty-one.

MOTHER: What are you talking about?

FATHER: Might as well fess up Looie. We've got you dead to rights.

MOTHER: I'm afraid you've lost me.

FATHER: Are you going to stand there with your bare face hanging out and tell this court you never heard of Richard F. Davenport? Red hair, freckles, moustache?

MOTHER: Science.

FATHER: A light dawns.

MOTHER: Billy's science teacher in junior high.

FATHER: Go to the head of the class.

MOTHER: What about him?

FATHER: Indeed.

MOTHER: What's *he* got to do with Charlie Chan?

FATHER: She said innocently.

MOTHER: I can't keep up with you.

FATHER: Flattery will get you nowhere.

MOTHER: One minute it's the Hubbard boy and Charlie Chan—

FATHER: —*"The Dissection Caper"*—*nineteen sixty-one.*

MOTHER: If that's a Chan picture I never saw it.

FATHER: Sure you did.

MOTHER: I don't remember.

FATHER: This science teacher, played by Richard F. Davenport, gives each kid in class a frog to dissect. Number One son, played by Billy, refuses to do it. *(Studies her.)* Do I perceive a glimmer?

MOTHER: Mr. Davenport told him he'd have to bring a letter from us requesting he be excused.

FATHER: Give that little lady eight silver dollars.

MOTHER: He said religion or nausea would be sufficient grounds.

FATHER: Which presented a problem since we practice no religion and come from a long line of strong stomachs.

MOTHER: I forget how it ends.

FATHER: I applauded Billy's reverence for life. I told him we both did. After all, didn't we loathe hunters, feed all the birds for miles around, forbid the killing of any living thing on our property?

MOTHER: We had Have-a-Heart traps to catch mice without injuring them. After breakfast Billy would turn them loose in the field.

FATHER: Feeling the way I did, it would have been the easiest thing in the world for me to write: "Dear Mr. Davenport. Excuse my son from dissection because we don't believe in killing." The easiest thing in the world. *So* easy that I said we ought to examine the matter more closely— see if there were any factors we weren't considering, any arguments for the other side. "For instance," I said to him. "What would happen if *everyone* took your position?" He said they'd stop buying frogs to cut up. I said, "What about medicine—surgery? Where would *they* be if everyone felt like you" He said he had no intention of becoming a doctor so for him to cut up a frog would be a waste. I said first of all it was a little early in the game for him to say what he would or would not be. And that went for the whole class. Some kids might discover they had a feeling for it—even *he* might. If no one did the frogs then that would leave a whole area of experience unexplored and if everyone felt that where would mother have been when she needed the delicate operation that saved her life. "I will not force you to a decision," I said. "I won't even advise you, because what you do is up to you. But no note to Mr. Davenport because that would be the easy way out. When you go against the tide, take a stand, you pay a price and this is as good a time to learn that as any."

MOTHER: Actually he came to *me* first. I was glad he felt the way he did and would have given him the note but I didn't want *you* to say I mollycoddled him so I told him I'd have to take the matter up with you. You took him to the study and had a long talk. I never heard any more about it. At the end of the year he got an A in science. I asked about the frog. He said he'd dissected it. He said it wasn't so bad once you got started. I'm sure the Kennedys had a reverence for life but I'm equally sure they dissected frogs without a qualm. *(The bell rings exactly as before—three rings, beat, three rings.)* I'm sure the Kennedys had a reverence for life but I'm equally sure they dissected frogs without a qualm.

FATHER: Without a quiver.

MOTHER: A reservation.

FATHER: A misgiving.

MOTHER: A hesitation.

FATHER: A regret.

MOTHER: A pang.

FATHER: A twinge. *(The bell as before.)*

MOTHER: A fear.

FATHER: A fear.

> *(The bell again. The pattern three rings, beat, three rings, repeated twice as the lights go down and the curtain descends.)*

THE END

SO PLEASE BE KIND

INTRODUCTION

The title derived from a song whose first line is, "This is my first affair—so please be kind."

A frothy bit that came to me on Fifth Avenue when my wife and I passed a well-known movie actor that only she saw but couldn't recall his name.

She ransacked her brain with me soliciting clues ("What pictures was he in?" et cetera) to no avail.

We tried to drop the subject but failed. Resorted to naming every star we could think of. No dice.

Suppose instead of my wife and I, it had been a couple enroute to an adulterous rendezvous.

Voilà. A one-act!

Preparing for a second production some years later, I found that many of the actors mentioned in the initial version were deceased or forgotten.

So I updated the piece with then current stars.

What follows are both the original and updated versions of the play.

As you will see, a third updating is now required.

All in all, an instructive lesson regarding the brevity of fame.

ORIGINAL PRODUCTION

So Please Be Kind was presented by the Ensemble Studio Theatre in 1972. The play was directed by Curt Dempster with the following cast:

A Man . . . . Biff McGuire
A Woman . . . . Lois Smith
Bellboy . . . . Gary Nebiol

Time: Present, afternoon. Place: A New York hotel room. At rise: A bellboy ushers a man and a woman (in their forties) into the room.

MAN: Robert Redford?

WOMAN: No.

MAN: Paul Newman?

WOMAN: No.

MAN: Warren Beatty?

WOMAN: No.

BELLBOY: Where would you like the bags?

MAN: Anywhere...David Niven?

WOMAN: He's dead.

MAN: I didn't know that.

BELLBOY: Died in Switzerland. Everyone thought he was English. Actually he was born in Scotland. Won an Oscar for "Separate Tables" in 1958. Would you like the air conditioning on?

MAN: No.

WOMAN: Wait!...*Darn.*

MAN: What?

WOMAN: It was at the tip of my tongue.

MAN: Sounds like?

WOMAN: It's gone.

MAN: Burt Reynolds is in town. I saw him on the "Today Show."

WOMAN: It wasn't Burt Reynolds.

MAN: Older or younger?

WOMAN: Than Reynolds?

MAN: Yes.

WOMAN: Older.

MAN: Any physical resemblance?

WOMAN: No. Reynolds is muscular—tougher.

MAN: This guy's delicate?

WOMAN: No.

MAN: What then?

WOMAN: He's strong but in a more sensitive way.

MAN: Like Richard Burton?

WOMAN: Burton's dead.

MAN: I know that. I was just giving an example.

BELLBOY: He died in Switzerland too. "Cleopatra," "Virginia Woolf," "The

Desert Rats." He was some actor, Burton, although a lot of people say he never realized his full potential.

WOMAN: You're a movie buff.

BELLBOY: First class.

WOMAN: Maybe you could help us: We just passed an actor in the street and it's driving us crazy we can't think of his name.

BELLBOY: What pictures was he in?

WOMAN: Lots but I can't think of a particular one.

BELLBOY: *(To the man.)* Describe him.

MAN: I didn't see his face.

WOMAN: I did. *(She measures a yard with her hands.)* This close.

BELLBOY: Good looking?

WOMAN: Yes. But not like Cary Grant or Gable.

BELLBOY: Off-beat like Bogart?

WOMAN: Yes.

BELLBOY: We're talking star?

WOMAN: Yes.

BELLBOY: What magnitude?

WOMAN: Magnitude?

BELLBOY: Is he a super star, medium, minor?

WOMAN: I'd say medium.

BELLBOY: Height?

MAN: Six foot.

BELLBOY: I thought you didn't see him.

MAN: Not his face but from the rear after she spotted him.

BELLBOY: *(To the woman.)* What sort of roles does he play?

WOMAN: You name it.

BELLBOY: Comedy? Drama?

WOMAN: Yes.

BELLBOY: Both.

WOMAN: Yes.

BELLBOY: Westerns?

WOMAN: Yes.

BELLBOY: Cops and robbers?

WOMAN: Everything but musicals.

BELLBOY: Always the good guy?

WOMAN: No, but even when he does bad things you don't hold it against him.

MAN: Hold the phone!

(They regard him.)

WOMAN: Well?

MAN: *Clint Eastwood.*

WOMAN: No.

BELLBOY: Eastwood is a *super*star. She said medium.

MAN: Pardon me.

BELLBOY: How long since you saw him in a picture?

WOMAN: A while.

BELLBOY: One year? Two?

WOMAN: I don't remember.

BELLBOY: Five years? Ten?

MAN: She said she doesn't remember. *(Hands the bellboy two dollars by way of dismissal.)* Here you go.

BELLBOY: *(Accepting the money but loath to leave.)* Give me three minutes I guarantee I get it.

MAN: *(Indicating the door.)* We have an appointment.

BELLBOY: Two minutes. I don't get it I return the tip.

MAN: *(Opening the door.)* We're running late.

BELLBOY: *(Starts to exit—stops.)* Did he ever do a TV series?

WOMAN: Not that I know of.

MAN: *We'd like to unpack.*

BELLBOY: One last shot?

MAN: No.

BELLBOY: *(To the woman.)* Please?

WOMAN: Go on.

BELLBOY: You hear me say the name, stop me. Okay?

WOMAN: Yes.

BELLBOY: *(Rapid fire.)* Brando, Pacino, De Niro, Hackman, Voight, Arkin, Alda, Bronson, Falk. Gazzara, Beau Bridges, Jeff Bridges, Lloyd Bridges, James Garner, James Caan, James Stewart, Kirk Douglas, Mike Douglas, Robert Mitchum...

(As he rattles on with no sign of quitting, the Man ushers him from the room and shuts the door.)

MAN: *Amen.*

WOMAN: Why did you stop him?

MAN: You're kidding.

WOMAN: He might have come up with it.

MAN: You're not kidding. *(He laughs.)*

WOMAN: What's funny?

MAN: We move heaven and earth to steal some time together and spend it trying to remember the name of some half-assed actor.

WOMAN: You're right.

MAN: Are we crazy or what?

WOMAN: We're crazy.

(Both laugh until he embraces her torridly, introducing a mood of serious purpose and mutual awkwardness as they separate.)

MAN: Well here we are.

WOMAN: Yes.

MAN: Alone at last.

WOMAN: Yes.

MAN: I never thought it would happen.

WOMAN: Neither did I.

MAN: Why don't you take off your coat—stay a while?

WOMAN: Don't mind if I do.

(He helps her remove her coat.)

MAN: I feel like a kid on his first date.

WOMAN: For me in a way it is. I've never done this before—been unfaithful.

MAN: I know.

WOMAN: How?

MAN: I just know.

WOMAN: How many times have *you* been unfaithful?

MAN: Do you have to put it that way?

WOMAN: How many affairs, liaisons, escapades—take your pick have you had?

MAN: What difference does it make?

WOMAN: Want to know what I think?

MAN: No.

(He would take her in his arms, but she stops him.)

WOMAN: You don't want to know what I think? You just want to jump in bed?

MAN: Of course not. What do you think?

WOMAN: It's your first time too. And before you deny it out of some macho compulsion remember this could be the start of something wonderful if we're honest with each other… Well?

MAN: Okay.

WOMAN: It's your first?

(He nods reluctant assent. She embraces him delightedly.)

MAN: You don't think less of me?

WOMAN: Just the opposite: Being the first time for both of us gives the whole thing a sort of—

MAN: —Purity?

WOMAN: *Purity—yes.*

 (They embrace mutually.)

MAN: Ever since we met at the Eisenblatts I've dreamed of this moment.

WOMAN: Me too.

 (They embrace again with growing ardor.)

MAN: The nights I made love to Estelle, I pretended it was you.

WOMAN: I did the same with Ben.

MAN: *(Nibbling her ears, her neck.)* I want to possess you totally.

WOMAN: Yes.

MAN: I want to know everything about you.

WOMAN: Yes.

MAN: Tell me what you're thinking.

WOMAN: He's not half-assed.

MAN: What?

WOMAN: The actor we passed.

MAN: What about him?

WOMAN: You said he was "half-assed." He's not.

 (He breaks contact.)

WOMAN: You asked me what I was thinking.

MAN: According to my watch it's two-forty. Your train leaves at five. That means we have two hours and twenty minutes.

WOMAN: It wasn't my idea to stop for lunch.

MAN: You seemed nervous. I didn't want to rush you.

WOMAN: That was very considerate.

MAN: Thanks.

WOMAN: *(Moving to him.)* I mean it.

 (He remains petulant and passive. She kisses him.)

WOMAN: I remember you now: You're that fascinating man who kissed me in the Eisenblatt's kitchen... *(Kisses him again.)* The Berger's closet...
 (She continues caressing him—he starts to respond.)

WOMAN: The Freeman's laundry room...

MAN: The Kelly's attic...

WOMAN: The Simpson's pool house...

MAN: The Irving's greenhouse...

WOMAN: The Peterson's garage...
 (She waits for his answering line. He doesn't offer it.)

WOMAN: The Peterson's garage...
 (Still no response. She realizes he's withdrawn from the game.)

WOMAN: What's the matter?

MAN: Nothing.

WOMAN: You stopped.

MAN: The Irving's greenhouse.

WOMAN: You said that.

MAN: *Robert Duvall.*

WOMAN: What?

MAN: Robert Duvall plays all kinds of parts and when he kills people you don't dislike him. Was it Robert Duvall?

WOMAN: No! And it wasn't Anthony Perkins, Glenn Ford, Elliot Gould or Richard Dreyfus.

MAN: How about Richard Gere, Robert Wagner, Richard Chamberlain, Richard Widmark, Gene Wilder?

WOMAN: No. Feel better?

MAN: Yes. How about you?

WOMAN: Yes. Where were we?

MAN: Something like this.

(He embraces her. She responds. They move to the bed; collapse upon it, are grappling feverishly when the phone rings. They cease activity—sit up. Another ring.)

MAN: Did you tell anyone where you'd be?

WOMAN: No. Did you?

MAN: No.

(Another ring.)

WOMAN: Probably a wrong number.

MAN: Probably.

(Ring.)

WOMAN: Maybe it's the house detective.

MAN: In this day and age?

(Ring.)

WOMAN: Suppose it was a fire and they were trying to warn us.

(That does it. He picks up the receiver.)

MAN: Hello…Yes… *(Covers the mouthpiece—turns to the woman.)* It's the bellboy. He wants to know if the actor was British.

WOMAN: No.

MAN: *(On the phone.)* She says no…Look we appreciate your help but the game is over. *(He hangs up.)* Incredible.

WOMAN: *(Preoccupied.)* What?

MAN: Him calling to ask if the guy was British. *(Dials operator.)* No calls till further notice…Thank you. *(Hangs up.)* Talk about timing.

WOMAN: He *might* have been British.

MAN: You just said he wasn't.

WOMAN: Now I'm not sure. Did he look British from the rear?

MAN: Did who look British?

WOMAN: The actor we passed.

MAN: What actor we passed?

WOMAN: I get it: We're washing it out of our minds.

MAN: It never happened.

WOMAN: From this moment, the subject is taboo.

MAN: Erased.

WOMAN: Eradicated.

MAN: Banished.

(They embrace—passion swelling.)

WOMAN: I can't tell you how relieved I feel.

MAN: Me too.

WOMAN: Mind over matter.

MAN: A little will power is all it takes.

WOMAN: We might have spent the whole time trying to think of his name.

MAN: Whose name?

WOMAN: It took place in England.

MAN: What?

WOMAN: Nothing.

MAN: You said, "It took place in England."

WOMAN: Slip of the tongue.

MAN: What took place in England?

WOMAN: *Nothing.*

MAN: Something took place in England or you wouldn't have said it.

WOMAN: Okay. The first time I saw him was in a picture with an English setting.

(He moves away angrily.)

WOMAN: I'm sorry.

MAN: *"The subject is taboo. Erased. Banished."* REMEMBER?

(His raised voice reduces her to tears, which makes him immediately apologetic.)

MAN: I'm sorry. It's just that it's almost three o'clock.

WOMAN: Why do I let such a dumb thing distract me?

MAN: I shouldn't have hollered.

WOMAN: Forgive me?

MAN: There's nothing to forgive.

(She would embrace him gratefully. But he holds her off.)

MAN: First tell me everything you remember about that movie to insure against further interruptions.

WOMAN: There isn't much to tell: It took place in England and... *(She remembers something else.)*

MAN: What is it?

WOMAN: *It was a war movie.*

MAN: Which war?

WOMAN: World War II. I see uniforms.

MAN: English or American?

WOMAN: Both.

MAN: Do you remember the story?

WOMAN: No.

MAN: The title?

WOMAN: No.

MAN: Just World War II, England, and he was the star.

WOMAN: He wasn't the star.

MAN: You said he was a star.

WOMAN: Later in his career. In that picture he was only a supporting player which is why I remember it because he stood out.

MAN: Anything else?

WOMAN: ...That's it.

MAN: Sure?

WOMAN: Positive.

MAN: World War II. England. Black and white. Supporting player. Could be English—could be American. Not much to go on.

WOMAN: Agreed. Case closed and thanks for being so understanding.

MAN: If he *was* English it would certainly narrow the field.

WOMAN: *Case closed—kiss me.*

MAN: Outside of Gielgud, Michael Caine and a few others, how many British actors do you know?

WOMAN: I see.

MAN: See what?

WOMAN: You've lost interest—don't want me any more.

MAN: Of course I do. But I'm not a faucet. You said he might be English. I say deal with it now: Name every English actor we can think of till we come up with it or exhaust the subject once and for all.

WOMAN: By English you mean Irish too?

MAN: The entire British Isles. Was it Albert Finney? Peter O'Toole?

WOMAN: No. Nor was it Alan Bates or Dudley Moore?

MAN: Peter Ustinov?

WOMAN: No.

MAN: Tom Courteney?

WOMAN: No.

MAN: You go.

WOMAN: Not Sean Connery. Not Richard Attenborough.

MAN: Alec Guinness?

WOMAN: He's way in his seventies.

MAN: Just say yes or no.

WOMAN: No.

MAN: How about double o seven? Not Connery—the other one.

WOMAN: Roger Moore—no… Go on.

MAN: I'm running out.

WOMAN: It wasn't Richard Harris… It wasn't Bob Hoskins. It wasn't Tom Conti…

MAN: Roddy McDowell.

WOMAN: No.

MAN: Did you see "A Room With a View"?

WOMAN: It's not Denholm Elliot.

MAN: That does it for *me.*

WOMAN: Me too.

MAN: You sure?

WOMAN: Yes.

MAN: *(Suggestively.)* Prove it.

(She kisses him. He responds. Passion escalates. He starts to undress her: Removes a garment, is removing a second garment when he freezes.)

WOMAN: What is it?

MAN: I remembered two more English actors.

WOMAN: I've got a confession.

MAN: Anthony Newley? Oliver Reed?

WOMAN: He isn't English.

MAN: What?

WOMAN: Just now when you started undressing me I had a flash. He isn't English.

MAN: Oh boy.

WOMAN: I wouldn't have said anything if you hadn't brought it up.

MAN: *(He sits—recites his mantra.)* Nom-Kyho-Bengay-Komo…Nom-Kyho-Bengay-Komo.

WOMAN: What are you doing?

MAN: Nom-Kyho-Bengay—

WOMAN: *What are you doing?*

MAN: Trying to stop my blood pressure from going through the ceiling. Nom-Kyho-Bengay-Komo…Nom-Kyho-Bengay—

WOMAN: It's a quarter after three.

MAN: Nom-Kyho-Bengay—

WOMAN: My train leaves in an hour and forty-five minutes.

MAN: Nom-Kyho—

WOMAN: *(Dressing.)* I was right: You've lost interest.

MAN: *Nom-Kyho-Bengay-Komo…Nom-Kyho-Bengay—*

WOMAN: That's the way you want it—fine with me!

MAN: The way *I* want it?

WOMAN: *(Grabbing her coat and purse.)* How much do I owe for lunch and the room?

MAN: *(Blocking her exit.)* Who spotted that actor?

WOMAN: If it's more than fifty dollars I'll have to pay you the next time we meet which can't be long enough as far as I'm concerned.

MAN: Who insisted on remembering his name? *Who?*

WOMAN: It takes two to tango.

MAN: What?

WOMAN: You should have put your foot down instead of encouraging me.

MAN: *On top of everything else I'm a wimp. Go. (He moves away, giving her a clear path to the door.)*

WOMAN: My last remark was uncalled for.

MAN: Nom-Kyho-Bengay-Komo.

WOMAN: I don't want it to end like this.

MAN: Nom-Kyho-Bengay-Komo.

WOMAN: Have it your way. *(She exits.)*

MAN: Nom-Kyho-Bengay-Komo…Nom-Kyho-Bengay-Komo…Nom-Kyho—

(A knock at the door.)

MAN: Who is it?

WOMAN'S VOICE: Me.

MAN: Now what?

WOMAN'S VOICE: It just hit me who the actor is.

MAN: Who?

WOMAN'S VOICE: If you want to know, open the door.

MAN: *(Opening the door guardedly.)* Well?

WOMAN: *(Going by him into the room.)* It's so obvious. I don't see how we missed it.

MAN: Tell me.

WOMAN: *Wayne Rogers.*

MAN: Hawkeye from MASH?

WOMAN: Yes.

MAN: When the bellboy asked if he'd done a TV series you said no.

WOMAN: I forgot. *(She twirls delightedly.) What a relief.*

MAN: What was the movie with the English setting where you first saw him?

WOMAN: I don't remember. But I'm positive it was Wayne Rogers. Aren't you glad?

MAN: Glad?

WOMAN: That it's over and we still have time.

MAN: You mean…

WOMAN: Yes.

MAN: From the top?

WOMAN: Yes.

MAN: The spirit's willing.

WOMAN: Leave the rest to me. *(She embraces him aggressively.)*

MAN: I thought Wayne Rogers was taller.

WOMAN: Don't talk. *(She is all over him; steers him toward the bed.)*

MAN: *(Coming up for air.)* How could you forget MASH?
   (Her reply is a shove that puts him on the bed with her above him. They grapple amorously until he thrusts her aside—sits up.)

MAN: *It's no good.*

WOMAN: What?

MAN: I appreciate what you're trying to do but it won't work. Not if this is to be the meaningful relationship we both want, which, as you said must start honestly.

WOMAN: I'm confused.

MAN: *It wasn't Wayne Rogers. And don't spend any more of the little time we have left saying it was.*

WOMAN: How do *you* suggest spending it?

MAN: By doing what we should have done at the outset.

WOMAN: Which is?

MAN: Meet the issue head on—confront it squarely. First order of business— clear the decks: Admit it wasn't Wayne Rogers. *Well?*

WOMAN: It wasn't Wayne Rogers.

MAN: Now we say the name of every American actor we can think of until we hit it.

WOMAN: And if we don't hit it?

MAN: Kismet. Ready?

WOMAN: Yes.

MAN: Go.

MAN: Martin Sheen. Jack Warden. Eli Wallach. Jonathan Winters. Bill Murray. Jack Klugman. Tony Randall…

WOMAN: Burt Lancaster. Jack Lemmon. Ryan O'Neal. George Scott, Jason Robards, George Hamilton. Stacy Keach…

(Lights down to signify the passage of fifteen minutes. Lights up finds them as they were, still naming names, but both just about tapped out.)

MAN: …Jerry Lewis?

WOMAN: No…Ditto Dennis Hopper.

MAN: You said Hopper before…Jack Nicholson?

WOMAN: Uh-uh…

MAN: How about Tony Curtis?

(She doesn't reply.)

MAN: How about Tony Curtis?

WOMAN: *Oh my God.*

MAN: It's Tony Curtis?

WOMAN: No.

MAN: What then?

WOMAN: I just remember where I saw that picture with the English setting where he made such a favorable impression.

MAN: Where?

WOMAN: The Loew's Paradise with stars on the ceiling and clouds that drifted. After the movie we went to Crums for sodas. I had a chocolate malted.

MAN: And the actor's name?

WOMAN: I don't know.

MAN: *Nom-Kyho-Bengay-Komo.*

WOMAN: But I know how to find out.

MAN: How?

WOMAN: I'll call Ben.

MAN: Your husband?

WOMAN: Yes.

MAN: What's he got to do with it?

WOMAN: He's the one I saw the picture with.

MAN: You're going to ask Ben?

WOMAN: Yes.

MAN: That's grotesque.

WOMAN: You're right.

MAN: He probably wouldn't remember anyway.

WOMAN: Probably not. It was ages ago.

MAN: ...If he did remember it would be a thousand to one shot.

WOMAN: A miracle.

MAN: Almost like a sign.

WOMAN: A blessing.

MAN: Do it!

(She dials a number.)

WOMAN: Ben?...In the city...I'll get the five o'clock...I don't know, I'll get something on the way home...We had veal on Monday...I called because a funny thing happened. I passed an actor on the street that you and I saw in a movie years ago. I can't think of his name and it's driving me crazy...I don't know the name of the picture. Just that it was World War II and set in England...Loew's Paradise...That's right—our first date... Right...Crums for a soda after—right...We did not—that was the second date...He wasn't a star then but we both predicted he would be... *You do?...* Tell me...Please it's important... *That's it—you're right!...* Thanks Ben...Me too...Bye. *(She hangs up.)*

MAN: Well?

WOMAN: The picture was "The Americanization of Emily."

MAN: I remember it: James Garner and Julie Andrews. Didn't we say Garner?

WOMAN: Yes. But it wasn't him.

MAN: Who then?

WOMAN: James Coburn.

MAN: Coburn. Of course. Later on he did those "Our Man Flint" pictures.

WOMAN: Right.

MAN: Coburn—what a relief.

WOMAN: Yes.

MAN: And we've still got an hour.

WOMAN: At least.

MAN: Nothing can stop us now.

WOMAN: No.

(They remain as they are. Lights down.)

THE END

'TWAS BRILLIG

INTRODUCTION

You'll find several plays in this collection that share a common setting: A writers' bungalow at a major studio in Hollywood where I did considerable time in the waning days of the studio system.

Why be coy? It was Bungalow 13 at Twentieth-Century Fox. Across the lawn from what had been Shirley Temple's studio digs at some point.

It has to do with blacklisting during the witch hunt days.

I'd always felt superior to those who gave names.

An easy and unearned superiority because I had no political past and by the time I arrived in Hollywood on this occasion (1958) the hunt to all intents and purposes was over.

I arrived broke (TV having dried up in New York) and scrambled for assignments. Sold an obscene number of shows in two weeks. All going splendidly when up jumped the devil via a contract from CBS that included a loyalty oath which I was requested to sign as a condition of employment!!! Exclamation marks because loyalty oaths were unheard of at this juncture.

My gut tightened.

I had a wife and child in New York waiting for me to earn enough to send for them.

I had nothing political to hide. I was a veteran of World War II.

To have my patriotism questioned was insulting. And I knew if I signed it I would feel forever demeaned.

What to do?

I called my agent (H. N. Swanson) and told him the situation. Like me, he was surprised that loyalty oaths were still in use.

"Sit still pappy and I'll get back to you," he chirped.

I don't recall how many hours passed before I heard from him, but it was an agonizing period.

The superiority I'd assumed over those who'd caved in during McCarthy's heyday vanished.

Swannie phoned.

"It's a hit or miss thing," he said. "Sometimes they send loyalty oaths—sometimes they don't. I'd ignore it."

I ignored it and that was the end of the matter.

I'd like to think that if push came to shove I wouldn't have signed. But until you're tested you can't be sure.

And that is how *'Twas Brillig* was spawned.

A là *Present Tense,* I could have written more explicitly but succumbed to ambiguity and obfuscation—the fashion of the day.

I was younger then.

ORIGINAL PRODUCTION

'Twas Brillig was presented by the Ensemble Studio Theatre in 1972. The play was directed by Curt Dempster with the following cast:

Edna . . . . Sarah Cunningham

Bob Kalmus . . . . Stanley Beck

Mr. Vogel . . . . Biff McGuire

Judith Kalmus . . . . Lois Smith

SCENE I

Time: Mid-morning. Place: A "Writer's bungalow" at a major film studio in Hollywood. At rise: Edna, the secretary, late forties, is tidying up the writer's office (her own desk is offstage) in anticipation of a new occupant. We hear a door open offstage.

A MAN'S VOICE: Hello. Anybody home?

EDNA: Mr. Kalmus?

(Bob Kalmus, mid-thirties, carrying a carton filled with books, enters.)

BOB: Good morning.

EDNA: I'm Edna—your secretary.

BOB: *(Offering his hand.)* How do you do.

EDNA: *(Shaking his hand.)* Pleased to meet you. This is your office.

(He surveys it.)

EDNA: Not elegant but I think you'll find it comfortable.

BOB: I'm sure I will.

EDNA: If anything becomes available in the main building, I'll let you know.

BOB: Don't bother—this will be fine.

EDNA: You're sure?

BOB: I like the lived-in look.

EDNA: I'm glad because I like it better here myself. No one bothers you. In the main building someone's always sticking their head in.

BOB: *(Looking out a window.)* Not much of a view.

EDNA: That's sound stage three. See that little cottage?

BOB: Yes.

EDNA: That used to be Shirley Temple's Cottage. Now it's some producer's office.

BOB: Is nothing sacred?

EDNA: This is your first picture.

BOB: That's right.

EDNA: I'm sorry to say I haven't read any of your books.

BOB: My fame precedes me.

EDNA: What?

BOB: I'm pleased to know that you know that I write books.

EDNA: Mr. Vogel told me.

BOB: Of course.

EDNA: If you'll give me a list of any supplies you want, I'll get them this afternoon.

BOB: Scratch pads, pencils and a three-hole loose-leaf binder.

EDNA: Lined or unlined—the paper?

BOB: Unlined. *(His attention on a weathered desk—feeling it.)* I like this desk.

EDNA: It's on its last legs.

BOB: That's why I like it. Everything else out here looks so new—especially the houses. I keep thinking "No one's ever died in most of those houses."

EDNA: A lot of people have died at that desk.

BOB: I believe it.

EDNA: F. Scott Fitzgerald had this office. So did William Faulkner.

BOB: No kidding?

EDNA: I worked for Fitzgerald. It was one of my first assignments.

BOB: Did he make a pass at you? *(Then hastily.)* Strike the question—I'm not myself.

EDNA: It's your first day—everyone's a little nervous the first day.

BOB: Thanks—you're very kind.

EDNA: Mr. Vogel loves your story. I heard him say so.

BOB: I bet you tell that to all the writers on their first day.

(They laugh.)

BOB: Fitzgerald huh?

EDNA: Yes.

BOB: *(Sitting in the swivel chair at the desk.)* He sat right here.

EDNA: The very same chair.

(Bob spins the chair—lets it come to rest on its own.)

BOB: Fair augury.

EDNA: What?

BOB: I asked the Gods for a sign: I said "If things are going to go well for me here then let me be facing Edna when the chair stops turning."

EDNA: But you're not facing me.

BOB: Don't be picky, Edna. *(Indicates the books he brought in.)* Four of those books are mine. That is to say I wrote them. If you'd like to read them, help yourself.

EDNA: Thank you.

BOB: If you enjoy them—tell me. If you don't—lie.

EDNA: It's a deal. Where are you staying?

BOB: The Beverly Crown Motel until we find a house. Fitzgerald and Faulkner, huh?

EDNA: Yes.

BOB: I'll cling to that.

EDNA: If you want me for anything just press that buzzer marked intercom.

BOB: Roger.

EDNA: And that thing... *(She indicates a small speaker on the desk.)* that's if you want to talk on the phone from any place in the room. You just press that switch. It's good if there's several people in the room who all want to be in on the same conversation.

BOB: Mother would have been so proud.

EDNA: I usually go to lunch at twelve-thirty. Is that all right?

BOB: Suppose I said no.

EDNA: I'd change it.

BOB: It's really a matter for the board but once in a while you have to stick your neck out. Okay—lunch at twelve-thirty.

EDNA: Unless you have something for me, I'll get back to my crossword puzzle.

BOB: How are you on old songs? Remembering lyrics?

EDNA: Try me.

BOB: *(Sings.)* "You ought to be in pictures."...What comes next?

EDNA: I know the title—but that's all.

BOB: I was in kneepants when that song came out. The words sounded to me like "You ought to be in pictures like anna rincheroo." I had the idea that there was a film star named Anna Rincheroo. Everyone thought it was very cute and they'd ask me to sing it and I'd oblige. Ever since I got up this morning that's been going through my head. *(Sings.)* "You ought to be in pictures like Anna Rincheroo." My question is what are the real words that I replaced with Anna Rincheroo?

EDNA: I could call the Music Department.

BOB: That would be cheating.

EDNA: Dismissed?

BOB: Dismissed.

(She exits into the outer office. Bob spins the chair again; rises.)

BOB: "You ought to be in pictures like dah de dah dah dah."

(The phone rings in the outer office. Edna picks up the receiver.)

EDNA: Mr. Kalmus' office...Who's calling?...One moment, please *(She buzzes.)*

BOB: *(Picks up the phone.)* Hello?

(No answer.)

BOB: Hello? *(Realizes he has the wrong line; presses the intercom button.)* Hello?

EDNA: *(Sticking her head in.)* Mrs. Kalmus is on the phone—press seven three.

BOB: Right.

(He presses the appropriate button as Edna withdraws.)

BOB: Kalmus Productions. Kalmus here...I'm here less than an hour—how *could* it be going? Hold it. There's a gadget I want to try. Hang on. *(He turns the speaker on; speaks into the phone.)* If this thing is working, it's like a loudspeaker. I'll be able to hear you and talk to you from any place in the room. Go on—say something.

JUDITH'S VOICE: Like what?

BOB: *It works.* Now I'm going to cross the room and speak. Don't go away. *(He puts the phone down; crosses the room.)* Damn said the duchess as she lit her cigar…Can you hear me?

JUDITH'S VOICE: Yes.

BOB: I'm all the way across the room.

JUDITH'S VOICE: Open the window, you can probably get Chile.

BOB: Now hear this.

JUDITH'S VOICE: What's it like—the office?

BOB: Shabby and worn. I love it.

JUDITH'S VOICE: Seriously.

BOB: Seriously. A little wooden shack. I think it's reserved for first-time losers out from New York so they won't get the bends.

(He waits but she doesn't speak.)

BOB: Are you there?

JUDITH'S VOICE: Yes.

BOB: *(Detecting annoyance.)* What did I say? Did I say something?

JUDITH'S VOICE: "First-time losers."

BOB: Sorry.

JUDITH'S VOICE: A moratorium on opinions: We're going to give the place a chance; no a priori judgments. Remember?

BOB: A slip of the lip.

JUDITH'S VOICE: What's your secretary like?

BOB: Very nice.

JUDITH'S VOICE: Anything for me to be jealous about?

BOB: We're on the air.

JUDITH'S VOICE: I've just come in from the pool. I'm about to have lunch. Then I'm off to do some shopping. I feel wonderful.

BOB: I'm glad.

JUDITH'S VOICE: Have you seen Mr. Vogel?

BOB: Not yet.

JUDITH'S VOICE: Be sure and thank him for last night.

BOB: Yes mother.

JUDITH'S VOICE: Stay off Truffaut, Fellini and Bergman.

BOB: Yes mother.

JUDITH'S VOICE: And above all—remember that one picture a year at these prices is the answer to all our problems.

BOB: I have it tattooed on my forehead.

JUDITH'S VOICE: As the great quack Doctor Rubin said "For you to get fired or quit would not necessarily be a victory."

BOB: I should never have told you that.

JUDITH'S VOICE: Bobby?

BOB: What?

JUDITH'S VOICE: I'm a little bit happy—don't spoil it.

BOB: I'll do my best. I mean that.

JUDITH'S VOICE: Thanks.

BOB: Actually, I feel pretty good myself. I drove up to the studio entrance. There were a lot of people waiting to get in—some kind of tour or something. They inspected me like I might *be* someone. I told the guard my name. He glanced at a sheet; gave me a big smile: "Go right ahead, Mr. Kalmus." The crowd fairly drooled as I entered these hallowed halls. Strike the word "hallowed" which betrays a sense of disapproval. Where was I?

JUDITH'S VOICE: Having a good time but expecting to be punished for it because of the awful way you treated your father.

BOB: I think my hour's up.

JUDITH'S VOICE: Hey, the reason I called is that that real estate man has some places to show us. Suppose I come by for you and we can take a look at the houses and then have dinner somewhere by the ocean. In fact one of the houses is right *on* the ocean—in Malibu.

BOB: I'll take it.

JUDITH'S VOICE: Wouldn't that be great—right on the ocean?

BOB: I'll have to ask Dr. Rubin.

JUDITH'S VOICE: You know seriously if you ever feel hung up at all don't hesitate to call him.

BOB: What time will you be here?

JUDITH'S VOICE: About six?

BOB: Right. I'll leave word at the gate so you can drive on the lot. That's how we say it here: 'on the lot.'

JUDITH'S VOICE: All afternoon I'm going to practice saying to the taxi driver, "Take me to Twentieth Century Fox, please."

BOB: You don't have to say please—we've arrived.

JUDITH'S VOICE: Have to run now.

BOB: See you.

(She clicks off. He hangs up; starts to settle in, is putting his books in the otherwise empty book case when he hears.)

EDNA: Good morning, Mr. Vogel.

MR. VOGEL: Good morning. He's in?

EDNA: Yes sir.

MR. VOGEL: Don't take any calls till I come out.

EDNA: Yes sir.

(Vogel knocks at the office door and simultaneously opens it.)

MR. VOGEL: Good morning.

BOB: Good morning.

(They shake hands.)

MR. VOGEL: I was walking—I thought I'd drop in. *(Regarding the office.)* Is this the best they could do for you?

BOB: Edna said the main building is filled but frankly I prefer this.

MR. VOGEL: I couldn't stand it for ten minutes.

BOB: That's what makes horse races.

MR. VOGEL: Well as long as you're content. But if you change your mind let me know because I want my writers to be happy.

BOB: It's a deal.

MR. VOGEL: The office may not be so hot but as far as secretaries go, you have the best.

BOB: She seems very nice.

MR. VOGEL: A jewel. Anything you don't know—just ask her.

BOB: I *am* a little disappointed.

MR. VOGEL: Disappointed?

BOB: I had visions of a nymphet who would sit on my lap and take ninety words a minute.

MR. VOGEL: Right now, your first crack at bat, Edna is better for you. The blonde comes later.

BOB: Blonde? What blonde?

MR. VOGEL: I thought you said "blonde."

BOB: No.

MR. VOGEL: "That's what makes horse racing."

(They both laugh.)

BOB: Before I forget: Thanks for last night. We really enjoyed it.

MR. VOGEL: The feeling was mutual. You know something? I get hunches about people and I'm never wrong. Right now, standing here, I've got a hunch we're going to do things together. I've got several ideas, properties that I've been keeping in the freezer until the right writer came along. I have a feeling you're the one I've been waiting for.

BOB: That's very kind of you, Mr. Vogel—

MR. VOGEL: —Sidney.

BOB: Sidney. Very kind, but I think I should make it clear that no matter how well this project goes I am a novelist.

MR. VOGEL: Don't you read McLuhan? The printed word is dead. But so what? You can do both—pictures and novels. A house here—a house in Maine or wherever. Maybe Europe even. A couple of the things I'm thinking about will have to be shot there. But this is all putting the cart before the horse. Number one, we have to do *this* picture.

BOB: Agreed.

MR. VOGEL: Edna will get you a lot of scripts. Some of my best pictures. Some of my worst. Read them all. The ones that interest you we'll screen. That will give you time to get settled—find a house and all. Next week we'll start to talk about the story. All right?

BOB: Sounds great.

MR. VOGEL: And don't feel obligated to come here to read. Go out to the beach. Get some sun. Swim.

BOB: My Puritan soul recoils—but I'll try.

MR. VOGEL: Incidentally, it's none of my business but if you see a house to rent that sounds too expensive, I mean if they want too much in advance, don't hesitate to call me.

BOB: That's very kind of you.

MR. VOGEL: You ever been to Palm Springs?

BOB: I was never west of the Mississippi till the day before yesterday.

MR. VOGEL: Of course, I forgot. Well I have a place in the Springs. We're having a few people down for the weekend and you and your wife are invited.

BOB: I'll have to ask Judith but I'm sure it'll be okay.

MR. VOGEL: If she has any doubts tell her Bob Redford and Gene Hackman will be there.

BOB: Sold.

MR. VOGEL: I'm trying to think if there's anything else…No, I guess that's it for now. Unless you can think of anything?

BOB: No.

MR. VOGEL: Then I'll be going.

(They shake hands. Mr. Vogel makes a move to go—turns back.)

MR. VOGEL: One thing.

BOB: Yes?

MR. VOGEL: What's the capital of the United States?

BOB: Come again.

MR. VOGEL: What's the capital of the United States of America?

BOB: I'll bite.

MR. VOGEL: You don't know what the capital of your country is?

BOB: Geography was my weakest subject.

MR. VOGEL: You think it's a gag?

BOB: It isn't?

MR. VOGEL: No…

BOB: Do you mind if we start over—take it from the top?

MR. VOGEL: What's the capital of the United States?

BOB: That's what I *thought* you said.

MR. VOGEL: Well?

BOB: Do I lose points if I ask what this is all about?

MR. VOGEL: Points implies it's a game.

BOB: Which it isn't.

MR. VOGEL: Correct.

BOB: Am I entitled to a phone call? *Wait a minute. (He hastens to the desk—regards the calendar—looks up disappointedly.)* I thought it might be April first.

MR. VOGEL: If you say you don't know what the capital is, I'll accept that.

BOB: Thanks.

MR. VOGEL: I know how the mind can lose the most obvious information in a crisis.

BOB: Is that what this is—a crisis?

MR. VOGEL: That's up to you.

BOB: "Twas brillig and the slithy toves."

MR. VOGEL: Is that it then—you plead ignorance?

BOB: *I don't plead anything.*

MR. VOGEL: I don't have all day.

BOB: What happens if I don't answer?

MR. VOGEL: You're fired.

BOB: Just like that.

MR. VOGEL: How can I work with a writer who refuses to answer the simplest question?

BOB: Once at a cocktail party I heard someone say "Life is a constant choosing between the lesser and the more." But in this case, which is the lesser—which is the more?

MR. VOGEL: I think we're beginning to get somewhere.

BOB: You feel that too.

MR. VOGEL: If it makes it any easier for you, think of me as senile—someone you're humoring.

BOB: Thanks.

MR. VOGEL: Or a dream. Tell yourself you dreamed the whole thing. If you ask me ten minutes from now I'll say it never happened.

BOB: You're too kind.

MR. VOGEL: And think of the chapter it will make when you do your book about Hollywood.

BOB: That's the best one of all.

MR. VOGEL: I can't wait any longer. What's the answer?

BOB: I forget the question.

MR. VOGEL: What is the capital of the United States of America?
(He waits but Bob doesn't speak.)

MR. VOGEL: Well?
(No reply.)

MR. VOGEL: I'm going to count to ten...One...two...three...four...
(The lights dim.)

MR. VOGEL: five...six...seven...eight...
(Blackout.)

SCENE II

Time: Six P.M. the same day. At rise: Edna is gone. Bob is alone in his office. He sits in the swivel chair lost in thought. Judith, mid-thirties, enters the outside office; calls toward his partially open door.

JUDITH: Bob?

BOB: In here.
(She enters the office.)

JUDITH: Hi.

BOB: Welcome.

JUDITH: *(Surveying the office.)* Be it ever so humble.

BOB: How does that song go: "You ought to be in pictures"?

JUDITH: Like Anna Rincheroo.

BOB: I mean the real lyrics.

JUDITH: I don't know—you brainwashed me with yours.

BOB: Something about Jupiter or Mars.

JUDITH: *(She whirls to exhibit her dress.)* How do you like it?

BOB: Very nice.

JUDITH: It's the most I ever spent.

BOB: *(Sings to himself.)* "You ought to shine as brightly as Jupiter or Mars."

JUDITH: "Very nice"—that's all?

BOB: *(Focusing on her.)* Turn around.
    (She turns.)

BOB: Perfectamente.

JUDITH: Really?

BOB: Really.

JUDITH: I can take it back.

BOB: *(With sincere but excessive feeling.)* You've never looked lovelier.

JUDITH: *(Flustered, she covers by acting flustered.)* Well gee mister, I mean golly, you sure know how to turn a girl's head.

BOB: The sun really agrees with you. You're glowing.
    (She goes to him impulsively, throws her arms about him, kisses him. He accepts it passively at first, then responds ardently.)

JUDITH: *(Pulling away.)* Slow down. I may be a country girl but I've heard how you movie fellows operate.

BOB: I'll give it to you cold turkey, kid: If you want the part, lie down on that couch.

JUDITH: How big is it?

BOB: I've never had any complaints.

JUDITH: I mean the part.

BOB: It'll make you.

JUDITH: How about billing?

BOB: You'll be underneath.

JUDITH: You better speak to my agent.

BOB: Who handles you?

JUDITH: No one. I'm a good girl I am. *(Notices his books still in the carton.)* When are you going to unpack?

BOB: You know who once had this office?

JUDITH: Who?

BOB: F. Scott Fitzgerald. My secretary worked for him. You know what I did? I pulled all the drawers out of the desk; felt inside; examined every nook and cranny in the hope that I might find a trace of them.

JUDITH: Them?

BOB: Faulkner had this office too.

JUDITH: Want me to put your things away?

BOB: I found a bottle of aspirin, several wads of chewing gum, and then, just when I was ready to give up, a note written in blood: "Life is short. Art is long." Signed Scott.

(She detects a danger signal in this, studies him.)

BOB: Under Scott's signature, there was another inscription: "You can say that again." Signed Bill.

JUDITH: What happened?

BOB: Faulkner's signature was—

JUDITH: —*What happened?*

BOB: In a word?

(She nods.)

BOB: I've been fired.

(Jolted, she sits.)

JUDITH: Fired or quit?

BOB: I said *fired,*

JUDITH: Why?

BOB: My margins weren't right.

JUDITH: Bob, listen to me. I'm trying hard, very hard, not to let go of myself. Tell me about it as simply as you can but no jokes or I'm going to crack.

BOB: We reached an impasse.

JUDITH: You and Vogel?

BOB: Yes.

JUDITH: About the story?

BOB: Yes.

JUDITH: But he loved it. He told me so.

BOB: He's had, quote, "second thoughts."

JUDITH: Since last night?

BOB: Yes.

JUDITH: He doesn't want to do it?

BOB: Not unless there are radical changes.

JUDITH: Such as.

BOB: Such as the ending strikes him as arbitrary and false. He wants Ralston to live.

JUDITH: What else?

BOB: Isn't that enough?

JUDITH: *What else?*

BOB: He sees no reason why Andrews can't be black.

JUDITH: Go on.

BOB: He wants the locale switched so it can be made in Spain with frozen assets.

JUDITH: Go on.

BOB: That's it.

JUDITH: Did you hear him out—discuss it?

BOB: The man wanted to rape my story. What was there to discuss?

JUDITH: You didn't discuss it.

BOB: There was no opportunity.

JUDITH: He just marched in—said it had to be his way or else.

BOB: That's right.

JUDITH: Cinderella had till midnight.

BOB: That's show biz. *(Hastily.)* Sorry.

JUDITH: I must say you take it well.

BOB: Would you prefer tears?

JUDITH: If Ralston doesn't die at the end, the whole story is meaningless.

BOB: Exactly.

JUDITH: Vogel struck me as crude, possibly vulgar, but not a fool.

BOB: You never *were* a good judge of character.

JUDITH: It doesn't make sense. It's crazy.

BOB: If you think that's crazy, wait till you hear the *real* story.

JUDITH: What do you mean?

BOB: What's the capital of the United States?

JUDITH: What?

BOB: What's the capital of the United States of America?

JUDITH: What are you talking about?

BOB: I'm talking about the capital of the United States of America. What is it?

JUDITH: Now look—

BOB: *—Don't play the fool! I asked a question—I want an answer: What is the capital of the United States?*

JUDITH: I don't know what you're doing or why but stop—*for God's sake stop.*

BOB: My very words to Sidney—Mr. Vogel: "I don't know why you're doing this but stop."

JUDITH: Vogel?

BOB: "If you don't *know* the capital of the United States—admit it," he said. "Plead ignorance."

JUDITH: Bob, look—listen to me...I *know* you're trying to tell me something important that I should be getting. But it's not coming through.

BOB: Vogel asked me what the capital of the United States is.

JUDITH: I'm sorry—I don't get it.

BOB: Sidney Vogel interrupted his morning stroll to drop in here; he welcomed me to the studio. He invited us to Palm Springs for the weekend. He asked me what the capital of the United States is.

JUDITH: Would you do me a favor? Would you let me call Rubin?

BOB: What for?

JUDITH: Because I don't think I can cope with this.

BOB: I got fired. I'm trying to explain why.

JUDITH: It wasn't the story? Because he wanted to make changes?

BOB: He loves the story.

JUDITH: Then I don't—

BOB: —Vogel, apropos of nothing, asked me what the capital of the United States is. I couldn't answer and he fired me.

JUDITH: *(Searching his face.)* You're not kidding. You mean it.

BOB: That's right.

JUDITH: Why?

BOB: *Why* did he ask me or *why* didn't I answer?

JUDITH: Both.

BOB: I don't know why he asked me. I've been sitting here all day trying to figure it out.

JUDITH: Why didn't you answer him?

BOB: Maybe his wife found me attractive and he wanted to deball me.

JUDITH: Why didn't you answer him?

BOB: Maybe he was one of those guys who caved in during the McCarthy era and wanted to give me a taste of what it was like.

JUDITH: *Why didn't you answer him?*

BOB: Why didn't *you* answer *me* when *I* asked?

JUDITH: I thought it was a joke.

BOB: So did I.

JUDITH: But later when you realized it wasn't a joke—why didn't you answer him then?

BOB: It was too late. There was too much at stake. I couldn't.

JUDITH: Wouldn't.

BOB: *Couldn't. (Touches his throat.)* It came up to here and stopped.

JUDITH: What was at stake?

(He regards her uncomprehendingly.)

JUDITH: You said there was too much at stake for you to answer. I'd like to hear *your* version of what was at stake.

BOB: My pride.

JUDITH: Go on.

BOB: That's it.

JUDITH: You want to hear *my* version? You want to know what *I* think was at stake?

(He just looks at her.)

JUDITH: I think our future—our lives were at stake.

BOB: Aren't we overreacting?

JUDITH: *I mean it!* Look at us. Married fifteen years. Pushing forty. And what have we got to show for it. No money. No home. Me still working.

BOB: *(Joking but not joking.)* We have four novels—not to mention our pride.

JUDITH: *You* have four novels and *you* have *your* pride.

BOB: I thought we were in this together.

JUDITH: —*Let me finish!* Most of all what we don't have, and what you promised me we would have, is a child. I want a child. In a few years it will be too late. You said it was just a question of money. Well this job meant the money. This job meant the child. This job meant a whole new life. That's what *I* think was at stake. So don't expect any medals from me because you didn't tell Mr. Vogel what the capital of the United States is.

BOB: You mean that?

JUDITH: Yes.

BOB: If I'd answered him, you wouldn't think less of me?

JUDITH: No.

BOB: Wouldn't harbor some buried indictment?

JUDITH: No.

BOB: Will you put that in writing?

JUDITH: So what happens now?

BOB: *Will you put that in writing?* That you wouldn't think less of me if I'd said, "Mr. Vogel, the capital of the United States of America is Washington, D.C."

(She studies him.)

BOB: Well?

JUDITH: You *did* it…You told him.

BOB: "The capital of the United States of America is Washington, D.C."

JUDITH: You weren't fired.

BOB: "The capital of the United States of America is Washington, D.C."

JUDITH: He's an eccentric old man and you decided to play along with him.

BOB: "The capital of the United States of America is Washington, D.C."

JUDITH: Nothing that happens here is real. You said so yourself.

BOB: "The capital of the United States of America is Washington, D.C."

JUDITH: A month from now we'll be laughing about it. I can hear you telling the story now.

BOB: "The capital of the United States of America is Washington, D.C."

JUDITH: *You didn't do it for yourself. You did it for me.*

BOB: "The capital of the United States of America is Washington, D.C."

> *(The lights, which have been dimming through these last exchanges, go out. Curtain.)*

THE END

COME NEXT TUESDAY

INTRODUCTION

Conception unclear. But it might owe something to Hickey's speech in *Iceman* about his wife who forgave the more he transgressed till he slayed her. Jason Robards punctuating his brilliant recital of the longest speech I know with two-handed double finger-snaps is a treasured theatre memory.

Unclear about *Come Next Tuesday's* origin, I'm sure of one thing it does share with *Iceman:*

Never before or since did I write such lengthy speeches as Lois Smith had to deliver.

Reading the play for the first time in ages, I was surprised because in the years since, I've prided myself on, and striven for, conciseness. Perhaps, at times, overly so.

It took a while but I finally mastered Jason's two-handed finger-snap ending with right palm striking left fist like a rim shot.

ORIGINAL PRODUCTION

Come Next Tuesday was presented by the Ensemble Studio Theatre in 1972. The play was directed by Curt Dempster with the following cast:

Louise Harper. . . . . Lois Smith
Harvey Harper . . . . Biff McGuire

Time: Tonight. Place: A living room. At rise: a husband and wife seated. He reads a magazine. She is pasting photos in a family album.

WIFE: We'll be married eighteen years come next Tuesday…Someone asked me the basis of a happy and enduring marriage. I said trust. Complete and absolute trust.

HUSBAND: *(Cocking his head.)* Did you hear something?

WIFE: No.

HUSBAND: A sound—like from the bedroom?

WIFE: No.

(He returns to his magazine.)

WIFE: "For instance," I said. "One night my husband came home late with lipstick on his collar. I said 'How did that happen?' He said 'The fellows at the office did it as a gag.' I never doubted him for a moment."

HUSBAND: *(Listening off.)* There it is again.

WIFE: What?

HUSBAND: A noise—like a window opening.

WIFE: I didn't hear anything.

(He returns to his magazine.)

WIFE: The next night we had some of the people from the office over to dinner. I could have taken one of the fellows aside and referred to the "lipstick gag." I just would have said "gag" period. If he didn't react I would have known you lied to me. But I didn't do that. I never mentioned the lipstick stains again. Why? Trust. One hundred percent trust.

HUSBAND: *(Listening off again.)* You don't hear anything?

WIFE: No.

(He returns to his magazine.)

WIFE: The same thing when those phone calls started: "Hello—is this the Harper residence?" "Yes." "Is this *Mrs.* Harper?" "Yes." "Well I think you should know that your husband is having an affair with Rosemary Landucci. Capital L-a-n-d-u-c-c-i of one thirty-four West Central Avenue." "Who *is* this?" "A friend who hates to see a nice innocent person like you who has given the best years of her life to a man being betrayed behind her back."

HUSBAND: *(Listening off again.)* Did you hear it *then?*

WIFE: No.

(He returns to his magazine.)

WIFE: Every day for weeks I got a call like that from that same girl. She'd always spell out the name Landucci: "Capital L-a-n-d-u-c-c-i. One thirty-four West Central Avenue." One night she said "You know where your husband is right now—right this very moment?" "Yes," I said, "He's bowling at the Fairmont Lanes." "No he isn't," she said. "At this very moment he's in bed with Miss Rosemary Landucci. At this very instant he's putting it to her. She's feeling good, oh so good. She's going to pop any moment now. Listen close and maybe you'll be able to hear." I heard bed springs. I heard moans. Then a woman saying "Oh yes daddy. Oh yes." And then a man's voice that sounded exactly like yours saying *"Go you dirty word, dirty word, dirty word."* It sounded just like you but I knew it wasn't you because the tone was savage, brutal, and you never use dirty words. "No," I said. "You can't fool me. That's not *my* husband." "Come on over and see," she said. "One thirty-four West Central Avenue— apartment five F."

HUSBAND: *(Listening.)* How about just now? Did you hear something just now?

WIFE: No.

(He returns to his magazine.)

WIFE: An hour later you came home. I asked how you bowled. You said you had a five hundred and eighty-one series—that the team had moved into fourth place. I asked you if you knew a Miss Rosemary Landucci. You said "no." That was good enough for *me*. I never even looked in the phone book to see if there *was* a Rosemary Landucci at one thirty-four West Central Avenue. That's trust. And it works: the calls stopped after that.

HUSBAND: *(Listening.)* There it is again.

WIFE: *(Ignoring him.)* The same when you started talking in your sleep.

(He goes back to his magazine.)

WIFE: You named girls—gave their addresses, phone numbers; described what you were going to do to them the following day—and where. I started to write down what you were saying when I realized that by doing that I was implying that I didn't trust you. I tore up what I'd written—put cotton in my ears. You don't do that anymore—talk in your sleep.

HUSBAND: *(Listening.)* I could swear I hear something.

WIFE: *(Ignoring him.)* The same when the anonymous letters started.

(He goes back to his magazine.)

WIFE: Letters naming dates, places, hotel room numbers. Letters including cuff links you'd lost—descriptions of your most intimate anatomy. I was tempted to confront you with all that but I didn't. "From now on, *you* open every letter that comes to the house," I said. "Pass on to me only those letters that you want me to read." That was the end of the anonymous letters.

HUSBAND: *(Listening.)* You're *sure* you don't hear something?

WIFE: *(Ignoring him.)* The same when that masked robber broke in. Just thinking of that ugly pig face mask he wore makes me shiver.

HUSBAND: I could swear someone's walking around in the bedroom.

WIFE: "Give me all your money and all your valuables," he said. "Or else I'll cut your heart out."

(He goes back to his magazine.)

WIFE: "My husband's not home tonight and he has all the money," I said. "And as for valuables, the only things I have are an inexpensive watch, some imitation pearls, and this engagement ring which you're welcome to." "You're lying," he said. "I happen to know you have jewels," he said. "And if you don't give them to me I'll cut your heart out." He had this big wicked looking knife and he put it right against my cheek. I tell you with that pig face mask and that big knife I was scared to death. "I think you have the wrong apartment," I said. "If it's jewelry you want, try the Hanleys in three B." "No," he said. "I'm in the right place. Where's the safe?" "Safe?" I said. "Yes," he said. "I know you have a safe." I started to laugh. "Oh yes," I said. "There *is* a safe here. It was here when we moved in. But we don't use it. You see the neighborhood used to be much fancier." "Open it," he said, and touched my cheek with that cold blade. "But I don't know the combination. We've never opened it," I said. "Where is it—the safe?" he said. I moved the picture on the wall and showed him the safe. "If there's nothing in it why do you hide it?" he said. "Because it's unsightly," I said. "What's the combination?" he said. "I told you I don't know," I said. "We never bothered to ask." He then took out a piece of sandpaper; filed his fingertips; put his ear against the safe and started to twist it back and forth. It was fascinating to watch. In a couple of minutes he had it. The door swung open.

HUSBAND: *(Listening.)* If I hear it again I'm going in there and see what's what.

WIFE: *(Ignoring him.)* "I thought you said the safe was empty," he said through his pig face mask. "If there's anything in there, it belongs to the people who lived here before us," I said. He reached into the safe and pulled out a pair of woman's panties. "What a strange thing to keep in a safe," I said. "The people who lived here before us must have been weird." "There's a note attached to these panties," he said. "It says 'These panties were worn by Rosemary Landucci, capital L-a-n-d-u-c-c-i, the first night she was layed by me' signed 'Harvey Harper.'" I must have turned a little pale because pig face said, "What's the matter?" I said "Harvey Harper is my husband's name." "What a coincidence," he said and pulled out a lot more panties from the safe. Each one had a note attached saying how and when it became a trophy, and the girl's name, and each note was signed by Harvey Harper. I said, "There must be some mistake. I know what it is: I'm dreaming." Well, I never should have said that because he came over and put that terrible knife to my face again—rested the blade against my adam's apple. The adam's apple isn't the face exactly but you know what I mean. "You feel that?" he said. "Yes," I said. "Then you can't be dreaming—right?" I had to admit it—I certainly wasn't dreaming. "But this is terrible," I said to him. "This is a tragedy; I've trusted my husband implicitly for years and years. And now to see those panties—well, it's a tragedy." "You ain't seen nothing yet," pig face said. With that he pulled out carbon copies of letters that Harvey had written to all those girls. Pig face read some of them to me. They were full of terrible things about me—just terrible things. I said I didn't believe Harvey had written them and he showed me the handwriting. It was Harvey's all right. And then he took out a viewer for thirty-five millimeter slides and had me look at some slides that were in the safe. Well, the things Harvey was doing with those girls. Well I had to stop looking because I was about to throw up. Actually I said something like, "It's the end of Harvey and me." And then I fainted. When I woke up pig face was gone. I was in a terrible state. All that lurid filth, the pictures, the panties, they were all over the floor. Well I thought I'll just sit here and wait for Harvey to come home. When he opens that door and sees it, he'll know we're through. So I sat there and I waited. And as I waited I thought about what a fool I'd been to trust him all these years. And then another thought came to me: Anybody can trust the innocent but it takes real faith, real love to trust the guilty. And then I had another thought: It isn't what a woman knows that wrecks a marriage—it's what her husband *wants* her to know. As long as a man is discreet he's telling his wife that he wants their marriage to last. Once he stops being discreet then he's saying he wants out but that he doesn't have the courage to say so. Well Harvey was certainly discreet. Could *he* help it if some sadistic pig face thief broke in here and exposed his indiscretions. If Harvey had been here when the thief arrived, he would have stopped him from opening that safe or died in the attempt. *Yes,* he would have sacrificed his life to spare me the pain of seeing what was in that safe. I could see myself at the funeral—crying "Oh Harvey you should have let him open the safe." Just thinking about it I realized how much I loved Harvey and that it would be stupid pride to let a sadistic pig faced thief destroy the beautiful union we've enjoyed for eighteen years—come next Tuesday. And what about our friends? When people say marriage is finished as an institution, our friends offer Harvey and I as a rebuttal. Was I going to let all those people down? I mean if Harvey and I ever broke up I know a dozen other marriages that would follow suit—the domino theory. And so I saw what I had to do! I gathered up all those panties and things and threw them down the incinerator. Then I closed the safe—covered it with the picture, and was watching Johnny Carson when Harvey came home. He asked me what sort of an evening I'd had and I said uneventful. He seemed to detect something wrong because he kept pressing me—kept saying he felt I was keeping something from him. I said absolutely not. I said everything was wonderful, never better. I said I loved him more than I ever loved him before. And I meant it. I threw my arms about him and kissed him. I can't recall being so passionate before. The next thing you know we were in bed and everything was wonderful. That was a week ago and everything's been heavenly ever since because Harvey and I have passed through our crucible—have weathered the storm. I know now that nothing in this world is going to end our marriage. *Nothing.* I can't tell you how good that makes me feel.

(Husband rises.)

WIFE: Where are you going?

HUSBAND: I heard something in the bedroom. *(He goes off into the bedroom.)*

WIFE: I probably left the window open and a breeze is rattling the shade…Or it could be the wood—old wood. Old wood has a tendency to creak so it sounds like someone's in the house…Or it could be his imagination. Harvey has a wild imagination. He's always hearing things…

(Behind her, unnoticed by her, a man in a pig face mask emerges from the bedroom brandishing a knife. Moves toward her.)

WIFE: Or it could be…Let me see now what else could it be?…

(Blackout.)

THE END

THE NEXT CONTESTANT

INTRODUCTION

Some years ago, I heard a radio show in which a young man exposed an ex-girlfriend to humiliation—she unaware his phone call is being broadcast. All this to win a few prizes.

Today, TV awash with people stampeding to debase themselves voluntarily, *The Next Contestant* seems antiquated bordering on innocent.

The repugnant folk who now bare all sign releases, while the young lady in the play, as in life, was never forewarned.

Who says things are getting better?

ORIGINAL PRODUCTION

The Next Contestant was presented by the Ensemble Studio Theatre Marathon in 1978. The play was directed by Curt Dempster with the following cast:

M.C. .... Sam Schacht
Walter .... Dan Ziskie
Katherine .... Melodie Somers

Stage right is a radio studio; stage left, a girl's room. At rise: A program is in progress. An M.C. is at the mike. The girl's room is blacked out.

M.C.: And now, on The Big Challenge, we bring up our next contestant, Mr. Walter Cartright.

(Walter appears, takes his place before the mike; there is applause from the audience.)

M.C.: How do you do? Nice to have you with us.

WALTER: Thank you; it's nice to be here.

M.C.: Where are you from, Walter?

WALTER: I'm from New York.

M.C.: What do you do for a living?

WALTER: I sell business machines.

M.C.: Have you any idea what we're going to ask you to do?

WALTER: No, sir.

M.C.: Well, let me tell you it's a beaut.

(Laughter from the audience. Walter smiles.)

M.C.: I understand you're engaged. Have a house picked out?

WALTER: Yes, sir.

M.C.: Furnished?

WALTER: Somewhat.

M.C.: Well, then you might be able to use a new Hydro-Surf Spray washer and dryer, a complete bedroom suite designed by Viking, a Royal console radio, TV and stereo?

WALTER: Yes, sir. We could sure use them all right.

M.C.: Well, they're yours, along with other gifts too numerous to mention, provided you meet your Big Challenge...Are you ready?

WALTER: Yes, sir.

M.C.: All right, here it is...We challenge you, Walter Cartright, to call up an ex-girlfriend who knows you're engaged and get a date with her. You can say anything you want with the exception you can't tell her that you're on this program or that you've broken your engagement.

(Some audience laughter.)

M.C.: Do you accept your Big Challenge?

WALTER: *(Hedging.)* Which old girlfriend?

(Laughter.)

M.C.: That's up to you.

WALTER: Where would I call from?

M.C.: Right here. From the Big Challenge Isolation Booth.

(A booth is wheeled out.)

M.C.: We'll be able to hear everything that's said by both of you…but you won't be able to hear us.

WALTER: I don't know.

M.C.: A Hydro-Surf Spray washer and dryer. A Viking bedroom suite. A Royal console. Plus the Big Bonus Jackpot…if you meet your challenge.

WALTER: Gee, I don't know.

M.C.: Well, let's get your fiancee's opinion. *(Looks out in the audience.)* Will Walter's fiancee please stand up? *(Spots her.)* There she is. And very pretty. *(To Walter.)* What's her name?

WALTER: Doris.

M.C.: *(To Doris.)* Doris, you've heard the challenge. Is it all right with you if Walter tries it?…She's nodding her head. She says yes. That's a game little girl.

(Applause for Doris. M.C. turns to Walter.)

M.C.: Well, Walter, what do you say?

WALTER: Okay. I'll try it.

(Applause.)

M.C.: What's the name of the girl you're going to call?

WALTER: *(Ponders.)* Catherine Horton.

M.C.: When was the last time you saw her?

WALTER: About a year ago.

M.C.: She knows you're engaged?

WALTER: Yes.

M.C.: Okay, let's get started. What's her number?

WALTER: Murray Hill 4-2325.

M.C.: All right, you go into the Big Challenge Isolation Booth and dial the number. Good luck.

(Walter enters the booth.)

M.C.: *(To the audience.)* Hasn't seen the girl in a year but remembered her number like that. Watch out, Doris!

(General laughter. Walter dials. The girl's room lights up. Catherine Horton, in her slip, is ironing. She does this in a vacant, listless, preoccupied way. The telephone, on a stand in her room, rings. She looks at it a moment; decides to ignore it, continues ironing. The ringing persists. The persistence of it gains Catherine's attention. She stops ironing, regards the phone. She goes to the phone, puts her hand on it, hesitates, then raises the receiver. The ensuing scene is punctuated by audience laughter.)

CATHERINE: Hello?

WALTER: Hello?

CATHERINE: Hello?

WALTER: Hello, Cathy?

CATHERINE: Yes, who's this?

WALTER: Walter.

CATHERINE: Who?

WALTER: Walter.

CATHERINE: Walter who?

WALTER: Walter Cartright.

CATHERINE: Walter Cartright?

WALTER: That's right.

CATHERINE: No, it isn't.

WALTER: What?

CATHERINE: This isn't Walter Cartright.

WALTER: Sure it is.

CATHERINE: No, it isn't.

WALTER: Why not?

CATHERINE: It isn't.

WALTER: Why?

CATHERINE: It isn't.

WALTER: Well, it is.

CATHERINE: No, it isn't.

WALTER: I tell you it is.

CATHERINE: It doesn't sound like Walter.

WALTER: Maybe it's the connection.

CATHERINE: Who is this?

WALTER: *Walter Cartright.*

CATHERINE: No.

WALTER: I tell you it is.

CATHERINE: No.

WALTER: Why not?

CATHERINE: It can't be.

WALTER: Look, you know Ronnie Parker?

CATHERINE: Yes.

WALTER: And Dot Finley?

CATHERINE: Yes.

WALTER: Well, if I know your friends, doesn't that prove I know you?

CATHERINE: I guess so. But it can't be you. I think I'm going to hang up now.

WALTER: Please don't.

CATHERINE: What?

WALTER: I said please don't hang up. Look, remember that time at the circus when the elephant almost knocked your hat off?

CATHERINE: Yes.

WALTER: That foggy night we went to hear Frank Sinatra. Do you remember?

CATHERINE: Yes.

WALTER: Well, how would I know these things if I wasn't Walter Cartright?

CATHERINE: I don't know.

WALTER: So that proves it.

CATHERINE: I don't know.

WALTER: Lake Tindale?

CATHERINE: Lake Tindale?

WALTER: We visited Joe Bathgate there. We went on a picnic and got lost. They were just about to send out a search party when we got back.

CATHERINE: We were too late for supper.

WALTER: So we went into town to the Log Cabin.

CATHERINE: We had barbecued ribs.

WALTER: We split a third portion. Then we went to that dinky movie. *Now* do you believe it's me?

CATHERINE: It *is* you.

WALTER: That's what I've been trying to tell you.

CATHERINE: But it can't be.

WALTER: Well, it *is*. How have you been?

CATHERINE: Fine, thanks. You?

WALTER: No complaints.

CATHERINE: That's good.

WALTER: What?

CATHERINE: I said that's good.

WALTER: I bet you're wondering why I called.

CATHERINE: Yes.

WALTER: I want to see you.

CATHERINE: Oh?

WALTER: How about tomorrow night?

CATHERINE: Tomorrow night?

WALTER: Yes. All right?

CATHERINE: No. No, I can't tomorrow night.

WALTER: Why not?

CATHERINE: I have a date with this fellow. That's who I thought it was when the phone rang. He always calls about this time.

WALTER: Then let's make it the next night.

CATHERINE: I can't. I have a date with the same fellow.

WALTER: Could you break it?

CATHERINE: No.

WALTER: Well, then you pick a night. Any night.

CATHERINE: This week?

WALTER: This week or next week. I don't care. Just pick a night.

CATHERINE: Do you think it's all right? I mean you're still engaged, aren't you?

WALTER: Yes, but it's all right. Doris doesn't object if I see other girls.

CATHERINE: I'll bet!

WALTER: Honest. She's very liberal that way. What do you say?…She's away for a few days.

CATHERINE: I don't know.

WALTER: Don't you *want* to see me?

CATHERINE: I don't think it's right.

WALTER: I just want to talk to you.

CATHERINE: I'll bet!

WALTER: I mean it.

CATHERINE: All right, go ahead.

WALTER: Not on the phone.

CATHERINE: Why?

WALTER: It has to be in person.

CATHERINE: Why?

WALTER: Because it does.

CATHERINE: Why?

WALTER: It's important.

CATHERINE: Well, I can't imagine what it could possibly be…You're not in trouble, are you?

WALTER: No.

CATHERINE: Then what is it?

WALTER: I just want to see you.

CATHERINE: You *really* want to see me?

WALTER: Yes. What do you say?

CATHERINE: I don't know.

WALTER: Come on, what do you say?…What do you say?

CATHERINE: …All right.

WALTER: When?

CATHERINE: Now.

WALTER: Tonight?

CATHERINE: You can't make it tonight?

WALTER: Sure. Sure, I can.

CATHERINE: Where?

WALTER: Wherever you say.

CATHERINE: The Zebra Bar?

WALTER: All right.

CATHERINE: I'll meet you there in an hour.

WALTER: Okay.

CATHERINE: In an hour. The Zebra Bar.

WALTER: Okay. It's real swell of you to do this.

CATHERINE: It's a pleasure, Walter. Believe me, it's a pleasure. I'll see you in an hour. Bye now.

WALTER: Bye.

(They hang up. The girl clasps her hands, clenches them tight together, brings them to her bowed head, stands rocking, eyes closed, in an attitude of fervent gratefulness and prayer. Walter steps from the phone booth. The M.C. leads him to the mike.)

M.C.: Is this boy an operator or is he an operator?

(The audience applauds and laughs.)

M.C.: Well, you certainly met our challenge. Now let me tell you what you've won.

WALTER: *(Interrupts.)* What about the date I made?

M.C.: You don't have to keep it...unless you want to.

(The audience laughs.)

WALTER: No. But she'll be waiting there.

M.C.: No, she won't. At this very minute, one of my assistants is calling her to explain the whole thing and for being such a good sport, she'll receive a Monarch clock radio. Now let me tell you what *you've* won.

(Catherine suddenly becomes very animated. She rushes about laying out clothes. She holds several dresses up to herself before a mirror. The M.C. begins reciting the list of gifts. The audience "Oh's" and "Ah's.")

M.C.: A Hydro-Surf Spray washer and dryer. A bedroom suite by Viking. A Royal console radio, TV and stereo. And the Bonus Jackpot! A silver service for eight by Brock. Your choice of wall-to-wall carpeting for any room in the house from the huge selection available at Morrow, Inc.

(The telephone rings in Catherine's room. She picks it up.)

CATHERINE: Hello? Yes, speaking.

M.C.: ...A marble top coffee table from Bowman and Fine.

CATHERINE: Who?

M.C.: An electric blanket by H.Z.

CATHERINE: What? I don't understand?

M.C.: A complete set of lighter-than-air luggage designed by Miss Warren.

CATHERINE: Yes? Yes? What?

M.C.: A Randolph automatic toaster.

CATHERINE: Please say it again.

M.C.: Two weeks all expenses paid at the beautiful Marlin Hotel in Miami Beach.

CATHERINE: *(Softly; sadly.)* Again.

M.C.: A Dekto movie camera to record your happy stay there.

CATHERINE: *(Pauses; devastated.)* Yes. I see. I see…

M.C.: And all because you met your BIG CHALLENGE!

(Lights down as audience applauds.)

THE END

DREAMS OF GLORY

INTRODUCTION

I've tried and failed at many things.

The disappointment, sometimes pain, ultimately passes.

What stays with me are one or two things I wanted to do but didn't because courage failed me.

Hence *Dreams of Glory.*

ORIGINAL PRODUCTION

Dreams of Glory was presented by the Ensemble Studio Theatre Marathon in 1979. The play was directed by Curt Dempster with the following cast:

Bill	Biff McGuire
Ada	Helen Harrelson
Ginger	Jo Henderson
George	Bryan Clark

Time: Summer evening—the present. Place: A country club terrace. At rise: two couples (George and Ada Brewster, Bill and Ginger Farley), late forties, evening clothes, share a table. The sound of an orchestra, in the Miller mode, from offstage. Bill pops the cork of a champagne bottle into a napkin.

BILL: Barely a whisper.

ADA: Bravo.

BILL: *(Filling Ada's glass.)* Voilà.

ADA: Merci.

BILL: *(Filling Ginger's glass.)* Voilà.

GINGER: Merci.

BILL: *(Filling George's glass.)* Voilà... Well?

GEORGE: What?

BILL: You missed your cue.

> *(George just looks at him.)*

ADA: Bill filled your glass.

GEORGE: Merci.

BILL: De nada.

> *(Raising his glass as do the women.)*

BILL: To the two nicest couples at the twenty-seventh annual summer dance all of which we've attended together except for the year we went to Europe and the time I had the mumps.

GINGER: Long may we wave.

ADA: Cheers.

> *(They look to George.)*

ADA: Well?

> *(George offers no reaction.)*

BILL: You're on.

GEORGE: To the two nicest couples at the dance.

ADA: Bill said that.

GEORGE: Long may we wave.

GINGER: That's my line.

GEORGE: *(To Ada.)* Let me guess—you said cheers.

GINGER: The fizz will be gone soon.

GEORGE: Bottoms up.

> *(They touch glasses and drink. We hear the orchestra conclude a number to applause. And then the Leader's voice.)*

LEADER: After a brief intermission we shall return. Don't go away.

BILL: Excellent band.

ADA: As always.

GEORGE: Isn't it amazing that in the twenty-seven years we've been attending these affairs, less the summer in Europe and the time Bill had the mumps, we've never had a band that was less than excellent.

GINGER: It's a tribute to the dance committee.

GEORGE: Or shabby standards.

BILL: Are you saying the band's no good? And if so by what authority?

GINGER: Bill has one of the best record collections in town.

ADA: And George got up on the wrong side of the bed. Ignore him.

GEORGE: The brass is weak, the reeds need tuning, and the drummer lags.

BILL: Thus spake Benny Goodman.

GEORGE: *The brass is weak, the reeds need tuning, the drummer lags.*

BILL: You win—they stink. Agreed?

GINGER: Agreed.

ADA: Agreed.

GEORGE: I didn't say "stink."

BILL: Raise your hand for a refill.

GEORGE: Last year's band stank. And the one the year before was even worse. These fellows are passable.

BILL: How would *you* know?

GEORGE: When I was sixteen I played with Tommy Dorsey.
    (The incongruity of the statement and the matter-of-fact way it's made arrests reaction for a moment. Then they laugh.)

BILL: Is that Tommy Dorsey the shoemaker on Elm Street?

GEORGE: Tommy Dorsey "the sentimental gentleman of swing." *(Again the sincerity of the pronouncement prompts laughter.)*

BILL: What did you play with him—handball?

GEORGE: Piano.
    (Laughter.)

BILL: No more booze for this lad.

GEORGE: Tommy Dorsey performed at our prom. His piano player was late so I played the first set.

ADA: Dreams of glory.

GINGER: If I were you, I'd get the car keys.

GEORGE: At the end of the set, Tommy Dorsey said, "Kid, if you ever decide to give the music business a whirl—look me up."

BILL: Sounds like "Golden Boy" with William Holden.

ADA: His father wanted him to be a violinist but he became a boxer.

GEORGE: He gave me his card with a private number written in.

GINGER: They laughed when I sat down to play. *(Raising her glass.)* Refill.

GEORGE: *Tommy Dorsey gave me a card with his private number.*

ADA: What's the punch line?

BILL: When he dialed the number he got *Jimmy* Dorsey who Tommy disliked and was always playing dirty tricks on.

(Laughter.)

GEORGE: I never called him.

GINGER: I'll bite: Why?

ADA: This better be good.

GEORGE: I knew my family, my father, would never approve.

BILL: That's not funny.

ADA: His father wanted him to be a boxer.

GEORGE: *That's* funny.

GINGER: How come we never heard you play?

ADA: Having achieved the pinnacle with Tommy Dorsey, he vowed never to play again.

GEORGE: Bulls-eye.

GINGER: *Boo—hiss.*

BILL: Ginger likes happy endings.

GEORGE: I married Ada—have four great kids.

BILL: And any day now will become the new president of Ridgeway Products.

ADA: We agreed not to talk about that till it happens.

BILL: Only kidding God.

GEORGE: Murray Hill seven-four-six-five-three.

(They regard him.)

GEORGE: Tommy Dorsey's number.

BILL: Don't look now but I think we've exhausted that gag.

ADA: Seconded.

BILL: In favor?

BILL, ADA, AND GINGER: Aye.

GEORGE: It's not a gag.

BILL: Ginger and I are thinking of Bermuda for Easter. You guys want to come?

GEORGE: *It's not a gag.*

BILL: Prove it. Go inside and tickle the ivories like you did with Tommy Dorsey.

GEORGE: It's been thirty years.

GINGER: Put up or shut up.

GEORGE: What would you like to hear?

ADA: Ignore him.

GEORGE: *What would you like me to play?*

BILL: How about one of the songs you performed with Tommy Dorsey?

GEORGE: All right. *(He rises.)*

ADA: And just where do you think you're going?

GEORGE: To tickle the ivories.

ADA: Down boy.

GEORGE: How about "I'll Never Smile Again"?

BILL: Fine.

> *(George starts away.)*

ADA: George.

> *(He stops.)*

ADA: I don't know what you're up to or why, but Mr. Ridgeway is in there and he isn't going to like it if you make a fool of yourself. It could affect his decision.

GEORGE: No.

ADA: What do you mean no?

GEORGE: There's nothing I can do now that would influence Mr. Ridgeway's decision.

ADA: *He's decided who's going to succeed him. He told you.*

GEORGE: Yes.

ADA: You didn't get it. I knew something was wrong.

GINGER: I told Bill when we got out of the car, "George isn't himself tonight."

BILL: After twenty-five years and all you've done for that company. It's a damn shame.

ADA: *It's an outrage.*

GINGER: I could cry.

GEORGE: So could I. As a matter of fact, I did.

ADA: We shouldn't have come tonight. Why didn't you say something?

BILL: At times like this, a person should be with those closest to them.

GINGER: What are friends for?

ADA: So Paul Stockwell, yea sayer and ass kisser par excellence is the new president of Ridgeway Products.

GEORGE: No.

ADA: Paul Stockwell didn't get it?

GEORGE: No.

ADA: Who then?

BILL: Don't tell me old man Ridgeway turned the company over to his nephew? Don't tell me it's Bertram?

ADA: Of course it's Bertram.

BILL: Bertram is barely literate.

GINGER: Bertram was chased from the playground for staring up little girls' dresses.

ADA: Once again blood proves thicker than gray matter. Bertram—*My God!*

GEORGE: Bertram is not the new President.

BILL: Who else is there besides Paul Stockwell, Bertram and you?

ADA: An outsider! The old bastard brought in an outsider!

BILL: Some hotshot from a totally unrelated field, hardly dry behind the ears, who dazzled him at a cocktail party.

GEORGE: Cold—very cold.

GINGER: Mr. Ridgeway changed his mind—decided not to retire after all.

GEORGE: Getting colder all the time.

BILL: He's liquidating. Selling the company lock, stock and barrel.

GEORGE: Frigid.

BILL: I give up.

ADA: So do I.

GINGER: Ditto.

GEORGE: Mr. Ridgeway summoned me to his office at two-thirteen this afternoon. I noted the time because I sensed he'd made his decision—the occasion would be historic.

ADA: Just say who it is.

BILL: The man's had a traumatic experience—don't rush him.

GEORGE: Knocking at his door, the usual two raps neither timid nor bold, I wondered if I would ever knock at that door again.

ADA: Why?

GEORGE: Crossing to his desk, steps rendered soundless by the deep carpet whose colors and design registered with unprecedented clarity, I sensed how familiar things appeared to those en route to the guillotine.

ADA: *You made up your mind that if you didn't get the presidency you were going to quit.*

GEORGE: Yes.

ADA: How could you without consulting me?

GEORGE: Arriving at his desk, I waited for Mr. Ridgeway to look up.

ADA: Kids in college, savings zero. You had no right.

GEORGE: *I waited for Mr. Ridgeway to acknowledge me!*

GINGER: *(To Bill.)* I think we'd better go.

GEORGE: And miss the denouement?

ADA: *The denouement is we're broke and you're out of work.*

GEORGE: I am not out of work.

BILL: You said you'd quit if you didn't get the presidency.

GEORGE: Correct.

GINGER: You realized that would be a foolish thing to do—changed your mind.

GEORGE: No.

BILL: I don t get it.

ADA: I think I do: George is the new president of Ridgeway Product. *(To George.)* Well?

GEORGE: I cannot tell a lie.

BILL: *You got it?*

GEORGE: I got it!

BILL: *He got it! Eee-Yow! You dog—putting us on like that.*

GEORGE: I never said I didn't get it.

GINGER: You said you cried.

GEORGE: I did cry.

ADA: *(Tearful.)* Because he was so happy like I am now.

GEORGE: I did not cry because I was happy.

BILL: Relieved. Weeks of uncertainty and tension and suddenly it was over.

GEORGE: Strike two.

ADA: How did Mr. Ridgeway, who hates any sort of emotional display, react to your tears?

GEORGE: It happened later—after he left for the day. I slipped into his office, the room I'd coveted for twenty-five years, leaped on the desk and proclaimed it mine—all mine.

BILL: At which point, overwhelmed, you commenced to weep.

GEORGE: Not yet.

BILL: *(To Ada and Ginger.)* Not yet.

GEORGE: Contemplating the changes and alterations I would make, I felt euphoria give way to the most exquisite melancholy I've ever known.

BILL: Prepare for tears.

GEORGE: I had striven for the prize too long and too hard. It would never justify the expenditure.

BILL: *(To Ada and Ginger.)* I think we're almost there.

GEORGE: Looking out the window, at the view that would have to sustain me for the rest of my working life, I remembered the night I played with Tommy Dorsey, and the card he gave me.

BILL: Once again from the Hotel Astor it's that sentimental gentleman of swing.

GEORGE: With moistened eye…

BILL: *At last.*

GEORGE: …I extracted the card from the corner of my wallet where, worn and folded, it had resided these many years. Decided to avail myself of Tommy Dorsey's offer.

ADA: I think this is where I came in.

GEORGE: Using Mr. Ridgeway's private line I dialed Murray Hill seven-four-six-five-three.

BILL: It's best to humor them.

GEORGE: After several rings someone picked up and a voice said "Lombardo's Music School—Professor Lombardo speaking." I said my name was George Brewster—that Tommy Dorsey had invited me to call this number. Professor Lombardo reminded me that Tommy Dorsey died in nineteen fifty-six—asked what kind of a sick joke I was up to. I assured him it wasn't a joke—that I was just trying to verify that the number I called had once belonged to Tommy Dorsey. "No" he said, "it's my number, the number of the Lombardo Music School and has been for forty years." I wondered aloud why Tommy Dorsey would give me the number of a music school. "Dorsey was a good friend of mine," Professor Lombardo said. "He used to steer pupils to me whenever he could." "Tommy Dorsey told me this was his private number," I insisted. Professor Lombardo chuckled. "I remember now," he said. "That's what he used to tell them so they'd be sure and get in touch with me. What's your instrument?" I said I played the piano. "Piano's my specialty," he said. "I can give you an hour on Tuesday at six. Usual rate twenty dollars but since Tommy sent you it'll only be fifteen." "I'm fifty years old," I said. "Better late than never," he said. "I haven't played in thirty years." I said. "It's like swimming," he assured me. "You never forget." He was telling me how to get to the school when I hung up.

GINGER: That's the saddest story I ever heard.

GEORGE: Quite the contrary. For thirty years I'd been carrying that card wondering how much more exciting and satisfying my life might have been if I'd called that number. As of this afternoon and my chat with Professor Lombardo I am rid of such doubts. Tommy Dorsey conned me. My life is exactly what it should have been. I am a happy man.

BILL: I don't suppose I could see that card.

GEORGE: Having no further need, I tore it up—scattered the pieces from my office window.

BILL: Why did I know he was going to say that?

GINGER: Because you're cynical—have no soul.

ADA: *(To George.)* I believe you.

GINGER: So do I.

GEORGE: Thank you.

GINGER: *(To Bill.)* Make it unanimous.

BILL: Why?

ADA: That's what friends are for.

BILL: Okay it's unanimous. Now what about Bermuda at Easter?

GEORGE: You're on.

BILL: *(Raising his glass.)* To the two nicest couples in Bermuda at Easter.

GINGER: Long may we wave.

ADA: Cheers…George?

GEORGE: Bottoms up.

   (As they touch glasses they freeze.)

THE END

REAL TO REEL

INTRODUCTION

The *New York Times* (Mel Gussow) called it "A malicious comedy about movies and criticism that edges close to real-reel life. Some might consider it too à clef for comfort."

I have no idea who or what he's referring to. If I did, I wouldn't say in this litigious age.

Of course there's no law against speculating.

ORIGINAL PRODUCTION

Real to Reel was presented at the Ensemble Studio Theatre Marathon in 1987. The play was directed by Curt Dempster with the following cast:

Sophie Brill . . . . Doris Belack
Gordon Rideout . . . . David Gautreaux

SCENE I

Time: The present, Manhattan, ten P.M. Place: Between Central Park West and Columbus Avenue in the mid-seventies. The living room of a second floor brownstone apartment. A window overlooking the street. Drapes, open now, that cover the window. Doors to kitchen, bedroom, and outside corridor. Books, newspapers and magazines, (NY Times, NY Review of Books, New Yorker, esoteric cinema journals, etc.) abound. Furniture worn—mirroring long tenancy. A collector's item of a typewriter on a card table. A woolen robe and flannel nightgown haphazard on the sofa.

At rise: the apartment deserted. Street light the only illumination. A key turns. Turns again. The door opens. Sophie Brill enters—snaps a switch that turns on several lights. Late forties to mid-fifties. Her intelligence is superior and apparent. Her energy considerable. Breathing in a way that suggests recent exertion, she fingers her throat solicitously. The coat she removes and the skirt and blouse revealed are excellent quality but make no concession to fashion. "No nonsense" best sums her.

SOPHIE: *(To someone we can't see in the corridor as she tosses the nightgown and robe in the bedroom.)* It's a mess but you're welcome.

(Enter Gordon Rideout, late thirties, in a jogging suit. His good looks combine shrewdness, curiosity, and a sensuality so self-assured that, like old money, its effect is heightened by the possessor's indifference.)

SOPHIE: I criticized a friend for moving out of the city because she was mugged. She said, "See how you feel when it happens to you."

GORDON: How *do* you feel?

SOPHIE: Numb. Violated. Legs like jelly.

GORDON: How's your neck?

SOPHIE: Throbbing.

GORDON: After you call the police you better call your doctor.

SOPHIE: It's nothing a cigarette won't cure. Mind if I smoke?

GORDON: Yes.

SOPHIE: All who feel I'm entitled? The ayes have it. *(She starts to search for a cigarette.)* Thank God the cleaning woman comes tomorrow. What am I saying? There's no cleaning woman. I'm a slob.

GORDON: You dial nine-one-one.

SOPHIE: I know the procedure.

GORDON: The sooner you call the better.

SOPHIE: I keep a pack for emergencies. But where?

GORDON: I often wondered what it looked like.

(*She regards him.*)

GORDON: Isn't this where you work?

SOPHIE: (*As she hunts for a smoke.*) How did you guess? Of course—the bloodstains. Wouldn't you know the one night I might have boosted my image by being seen with you the old bitch on the first floor who notes all comings and goings isn't there. If I don't find a cigarette I'm going to scream.

GORDON: Be better for you.

SOPHIE: Preachy-preachy.

GORDON: The phone call?

SOPHIE: I'll have to go there and study pictures.

GORDON: Mug shots—yes.

SOPHIE: (*Locating cigarettes.*) Amen. Where would you be if you were a match?

GORDON: Get away from the window.

(*As he closes the drapes.*)

SOPHIE: You're not suggesting?

GORDON: If you got a good look at him he got one of you.

SOPHIE: The way he was running he's probably in Scarsdale. You wouldn't happen to have a match?

GORDON: If he killed that old man mugged in the park last week and you're the only one who can identify him—figure it out.

SOPHIE: If that's to divert me from cigarettes, congratulations. Care for a drink?

GORDON: No thanks.

SOPHIE: A wee one to be polite like the officers of a Danish freighter I once traveled on who never let a lady drink alone.

GORDON: No. You did get a good look at him?

SOPHIE: Indelible.

GORDON: Where's the mask?

SOPHIE: Coat pocket. Cheers.

(*While she pours and downs a generous shot, he takes a ski mask from the coat she wore when entering.*)

GORDON: This could tell them a lot.

SOPHIE: Like he's not original. The hell with hand guns—stamp out ski masks. Does it still smell like cinnamon?

GORDON: I don't know about cinnamon but there's a definite aroma.

SOPHIE: As I yanked it from his face I felt doubly assaulted. His hands at my throat and the odor of cheap cologne.

GORDON: While we chat he gets further away.

SOPHIE: I thought he was lurking outside the building.

GORDON: It's a possibility. Nine-one-one.

SOPHIE: Refill? Thought you'd never ask. *(She downs an even stiffer shot than the first.)* I'll bet you had me pegged for a teetotaler?

GORDON: Yes.

SOPHIE: A person who risks their life in one's behalf is entitled to peek behind the scenery.

GORDON: All I did was scare him off.

SOPHIE: "Said Mr. Rideout modestly." Anything else besides my not being a teetotaler that contradicts expectations?

GORDON: I pictured you larger.

SOPHIE: Bird-like is the usual description with emphasis on the talons.

GORDON: If you don't call soon you'll forget what he looks like.

SOPHIE: Six three, two-twenty, Caucasian. Dented features suggesting a quondam pugilist. A right eye which seemed to leak from its socket. Was it the right eye?

GORDON: I only saw him from the rear.

SOPHIE: My right—his left. It was the left eye. As though plucked out and haphazardly repositioned. Ugh.

GORDON: A cinch to spot if he's got a record.

SOPHIE: Pea jacket like sailors wear. Denim trousers. And I think boots. Did you note boots?

GORDON: No.

SOPHIE: Leather soles and heels in any case. I remember the clatter as he bolted which had to be him since you're wearing sneakers. I'll say he ducked into the park.

GORDON: Why?

SOPHIE: A big, heavy man outrun a trim fellow in jogging clothes?

GORDON: That's what happened.

SOPHIE: And you a non-smoker. Tsk tsk.

GORDON: Just the facts ma'am.

SOPHIE: One of the passengers on that Danish freighter, a wealthy Count, fell madly in love with me and tried to get the Captain to marry us. The Captain, a friend of the Count's family, hid until the fever waned. If not for that Captain I might have my own fjord today or are they just in Sweden?

GORDON: What are you afraid of?

SOPHIE: A complete answer would take ages but bureaucracy, fear of contact with any and all governmental machinery, is high on the list.

GORDON: Want me to make the call?

SOPHIE: Not only courageous but considerate.

GORDON: Do you know what precinct you're in?

SOPHIE: "Noted Film Critic Rescued by Movie Star." The press will have a field day.

GORDON: Can't be helped.

SOPHIE: "On the eve of the opening of his latest film, actor-producer-director Gordon Rideout, jogging near Central Park, came to the aid of Sophie Brill, eminent movie critic, who has consistently loathed his work." It sounds like a thirties comedy: the proverbial "cute meet."

GORDON: I don't recall any comedies where someone is strangled.

SOPHIE: If I pan your newest opus, which I'm seeing tomorrow, I get the bitch of the year award. If, miracle of miracles, I like it, they'll say judgment bowed to gratitude.

GORDON: Minutes ago you were nearly choked to death and that's all you can think of?

SOPHIE: *You* can't lose: "Screen Idol Real Life Hero."

GORDON: I was recently at a Hollywood party where someone said you spent so much time in screening rooms you didn't know what was real any more. Lady there's a killer out there you might be able to identify.

SOPHIE: Jules Jerome.

GORDON: What?

SOPHIE: The person who voiced that trite notion about me at a dinner honoring Jimmy Stewart was Jules Jerome, née Lipshitz, producer of several all time grossers in every sense of the word.

GORDON: Don't tell me Jimmy Stewart squealed.

SOPHIE: Jimmy Stewart never arrived. Your hostess waited till nine-thirty before serving a rack of lamb so over-cooked it was given to the dogs and pizza sent for.

GORDON: Who told you?

SOPHIE: I had two eyewitness reports. The most detailed from lips that moments before pressed yours. I'll give you a clue: honey blonde, highly pneumatic, and reputed to give great cranium. Which, if your reputation is to be believed, should make for a short list of hundreds.

GORDON: Tina Verdun.

SOPHIE: The same. Would you like your ranking in Tina's pantheon d'amour vis-à-vis Nicholson, Beatty, and other seeded players?

GORDON: I'd like you to make that phone call.

SOPHIE: So public spirited, I had no idea.

GORDON: I don't want to read about some poor bastard killed by a guy in a ski mask the cops might have nabbed.

SOPHIE: A laudable sentiment which would be even more so if not for the two point six million you borrowed from Wells Fargo to complete your latest flick.

GORDON: Four people in the world knew that.

SOPHIE: And then there were five.

GORDON: Incredible. And that's why you think I want you to call—the publicity?

SOPHIE: Not an unreasonable suspicion given your homes in Beverly Hills and Malibu pledged as collateral.

GORDON: I'm beginning to wish we'd never met.

SOPHIE: How about by mutual consent no phone call to the police?

GORDON: The whole thing never happened?

SOPHIE: Isn't that what you said you wished?

GORDON: But it did happen and there's a guy out there—

SOPHIE: —Seventh.

GORDON: What?

SOPHIE: On Tina Verdun's priapic all stars you bat seventh after Ryan O'Neal and preceding Omar Shariff.

GORDON: Those bruises on your throat are real.

SOPHIE: I'll wear something with a high neck displaying just enough to suggest a lover got carried away. *(She replenishes her glass.)*

GORDON: The police won't pay attention if you're sloshed.

SOPHIE: As in other ways, you underestimate my capacity. Skoal.

GORDON: I'm phoning.

SOPHIE: On second thought he was black with an afro and scar from ear-ringed ear to snout. A pigmy of my imagination? Conceivably.

GORDON: You won't call—you won't let me call.

SOPHIE: Head of the class.

GORDON: How about if you leave me out?

SOPHIE: "Before she could thank him, Ms. Brill's savior vanished as anonymously as whence he came"?

GORDON: Yes.

SOPHIE: No.

GORDON: You think I'd leak it.

SOPHIE: Inadvertently. Tell me about your film kept so under wraps I've no idea what I'm in for tomorrow which usually augurs turkey.

GORDON: Or heightens pleasure by lowering expectations.

SOPHIE: Is that what you cling to in the wee small hours when visions of collateral dance in your head?

GORDON: Let's hear it for the good Samaritan.

SOPHIE: I thought noble deeds were their own reward.

GORDON: On which note, with a final request you call the police, I depart.

SOPHIE: Life again duplicating art.

(He regards her.)

SOPHIE: The powers that be go to so much trouble to bring us together and before the surface is scratched, as in your films when something promising is chanced upon, you quit the field instead of exploring.

GORDON: I thought—

SOPHIE: —You thought coming to my rescue softened me and tarrying might see the presumed edge erode. Wrong. I wouldn't praise a picture I didn't like if it was made by my mother.

GORDON: Ever have the feeling you wanted to go and then have the feeling you wanted to stay?

SOPHIE: Aren't you sorry you didn't let that gorilla finish me?

GORDON: And deprive myself of all the nice things you're going to write after tomorrow's screening.

SOPHIE: Is it possible you believe that?

GORDON: Is it possible you're trying to keep me here because you're afraid to be alone?

SOPHIE: Petrified.

GORDON: I think you are. *(Softens.)* Look I can stay till eleven-thirty.

SOPHIE: At which time duty calls to the arms of—don't tell me—Candy Canfield, Roberta Simon, Jessica Cotton, Marcy Dalton, or the latest in defector, some say defective, ballerinas, Natasha "Good-bluss Who-nited Stays" Sobelevsky.

GORDON: If you really want to know, I have a midnight appointment at the lab to check the print you're seeing tomorrow.

SOPHIE: Hey gang let's go to Cinema Two and see the picture that won the neatest print of the year award.

GORDON: Given a recent review in which you blasted the producer for failing to cleanse the screening room of popcorn odor, plus damning the projectionist for missing two changeovers, one can't be too careful.

SOPHIE: You read me—how flattering.

GORDON: Doesn't everyone?

SOPHIE: Yes, but few in the business admit it. Am I really so universally hated—not to mention Paramount, MGM, et cetera?

GORDON: Suppose I said no?

SOPHIE: I'd fear slippage.

GORDON: Your crown is safe.

SOPHIE: Is it true you have a dart board with my likeness: ears ten points— mouth a bull's-eye?

GORDON: Not any more.

SOPHIE: I've been replaced by Khadafi.

GORDON: I no longer regard you as an enemy.

SOPHIE: I *am* slipping. Either that or Wells Fargo is tightening the screws.

GORDON: Some of the things you said about my work eventually sank in.

SOPHIE: I see.

GORDON: No you don't. But you will tomorrow.

SOPHIE: Proof of the pudding followed by eating humble pie?

GORDON: Hopefully.

SOPHIE: It would have to be a quantum leap.

GORDON: It is.

SOPHIE: And little old me is responsible?

GORDON: Indirectly.

SOPHIE: I've been offered cars, trips, every bribe imaginable. But this is a first—being threatened with collaboration.

GORDON: What do you want from me?

SOPHIE: How about a good screw for a rave review?

GORDON: I thought you'd never ask.

SOPHIE: Alone with the man who, according to *Cosmopolitan,* populates more sexual fantasies than any other person in the world, wouldn't I be a fool not to exploit the situation.

GORDON: These are the jokes.

SOPHIE: Well what do you say? And before answering consider that rejection by one who'd diddle the proverbial snake, not to mention Tina Verdun, would not be taken kindly.

GORDON: Is it possible you're serious?

SOPHIE: What do you think? More to the point: What do you hope?

GORDON: No.

SOPHIE: You'd hate to see me violate my integrity.

GORDON: That's part of it.

SOPHIE: And the rest? Let me guess: You have an aversion to humping unappealing older women.

GORDON: I don't find you unappealing.

SOPHIE: Fifty percent isn't bad. In what way not unappealing?

GORDON: I have a thing for intelligence.

SOPHIE: Dear God, just once before I die, let me be praised for tits, legs, ass.

GORDON: You want to be lied to?

SOPHIE: Passionately.

GORDON: I couldn't do that.

SOPHIE: I know—I've seen your work.

GORDON: It's not an acting problem.

SOPHIE: What do you bet Olivier could say I had great boobs, great gams, and not only make me believe it but a jam packed audience as well.

GORDON: With all due respect—fuck Olivier.

SOPHIE: He can't do you any good. I can. E equals MC squared. The capital of Mongolia is Ulan Bator. Am I getting to you?

GORDON: I said intelligence not information.

(The phone rings…rings again.)

GORDON: Aren't you going to answer?

SOPHIE: Interrupt a once in a lifetime dream?

(The ringing ceases.)

SOPHIE: Your move.

GORDON: I was about to leave.

SOPHIE: I was about to suggest the bedroom.

GORDON: Why do I think if I made a pass you'd scream?

SOPHIE: "With his latest picture, Gordon Rideout, scoring a triple coup as producer, director and leading man, compels me to take back every rotten thing I ever wrote about him." *Or:* "With his latest picture, Gordon Rideout reconfirms he is a tedious actor whose leaden deficiencies, et cetera."

GORDON: I like the first one.

SOPHIE: You still think I'm kidding.

GORDON: Yes.

SOPHIE: Try me.

GORDON: You're making me uncomfortable.

SOPHIE: That's encouraging.

GORDON: You happen to be someone I admire.

SOPHIE: Along with Margaret Thatcher and who else?

GORDON: Why do you tear yourself down?

SOPHIE: Is it possible your quest for the ultimate nooky is on the wane?

GORDON: You've found me out.

SOPHIE: You should have come to me sooner.

GORDON: You have a cure?

SOPHIE: Think Wells Fargo and the mounting interest on your loan.

GORDON: Don't look now but I'm beginning to enjoy this game.

SOPHIE: Sell it to yourself any way you like but don't take too long. The offer could be withdrawn at—

(He embraces her stunningly—holds her captive.)

GORDON: Reprise the terms.

SOPHIE: You know.

GORDON: I want to be sure.

SOPHIE: You're hurting my arm.

GORDON: Good screw—good review?

SOPHIE: Yes.

GORDON: No qualms about hating yourself in the morning?

SOPHIE: I always hate myself in the morning. It will be nice to have a reason.

(He would kiss her again but she breaks away.)

SOPHIE: I prefer the bedroom.

GORDON: What's the rush?

SOPHIE: Your eleven-thirty appointment.

GORDON: It will keep. Sit.

SOPHIE: I don't like being ordered.

GORDON: I know. Sit.

SOPHIE: If you're trying to provoke me in the hope I'll throw you out, be careful—you might succeed.

GORDON: Why would I hope that?

SOPHIE: You don't believe I'll keep my part of the bargain.

GORDON: I trust you completely. But even if I was sure you'd renege I'd go through with it.

SOPHIE: Why?

GORDON: I want you.

SOPHIE: For myself alone?

GORDON: Yes.

SOPHIE: Wells Fargo no part of the equation?

GORDON: That's right.

SOPHIE: Be still my heart.

GORDON: I mean it.

SOPHIE: I wouldn't pursue this line.

GORDON: 'Nough said. *(He indicates the bedroom.)* Shall we?

SOPHIE: Admit you're doing it for the review.

GORDON: What's the difference?

SOPHIE: What pride I take in my life derives from an absence of bullshit.

GORDON: Once again you underestimate yourself.

SOPHIE: Last warning.

GORDON: *(Hand raised in boy scout pledge.)* I'm doing it for the review and no other reason.

SOPHIE: You better go.

GORDON: Cold feet?

SOPHIE: I will not be mocked.

GORDON: That wasn't the intention.

SOPHIE: Guaranteed a favorable review right now, your passion wouldn't cool?

GORDON: Right.

SOPHIE: When the hundred most desirable women in the city, not to mention Ms. Sobolevsky, are panting for your call?

GORDON: Yes.

SOPHIE: How dare you treat me like some mindless twit.

GORDON: You really don't want to go through with it.

SOPHIE: Don't you wish.

GORDON: *(He embraces her fiercely.)* The time has come the walrus said. *(His hands roam her body till beside herself she speaks.)*

SOPHIE: Exterior. Aerial shot. A lake with four coves giving the appearance of a lucky clover.

GORDON: *(Breaking off.)* What?

SOPHIE: Isn't that how it begins—your film?

GORDON: Who told you?

SOPHIE: No one.

GORDON: You got your hands on the script.

SOPHIE: Better than that. I've seen it.

GORDON: No way.

SOPHIE: Kids scuba diving at a summer resort discover a car submerged thirty years containing a skeleton.

GORDON: There are only two prints both under lock and key.

SOPHIE: Plus the new one the lab made today which is excellent.

GORDON: The lab showed you my picture?

SOPHIE: Unbeknownst to anyone in a position of authority.

GORDON: How?

SOPHIE: Reveal sources? Never.

GORDON: Why, when you were due to see it tomorrow?

SOPHIE: Because, as you know, it would have made me miss this week's issue.

GORDON: And the thought of not being in on the kill was more than you could bear. Jules Jerome was right: You're consumed.

SOPHIE: Aren't you going to ask my opinion?

GORDON: I don't have to.

SOPHIE: Where's all that confidence?

GORDON: I should have let that guy strangle you.

SOPHIE: I especially wanted to see it because I'd heard rumors of quality.

GORDON: Your obituary and the review would have balanced nicely.

SOPHIE: I was keenly disappointed.

GORDON: We aim to please.

SOPHIE: Contrary to hopes and expectations, I liked it.

GORDON: I must have been whacko to...What did you say?

SOPHIE: I liked it.

GORDON: Liked it?

SOPHIE: Your picture.

GORDON: You liked my picture?

SOPHIE: More than liked it.

GORDON: You wouldn't kid a guy who saved your life and owes a ton plus the Wells Fargo loan?

SOPHIE: It's the best American film I've seen in ages.

GORDON: But?

SOPHIE: No buts.

GORDON: That's what you're going to write?

SOPHIE: Have written...You're not convinced.

GORDON: Believe me I'm trying.

(She goes to the phone; turns on the speaker, dials. Several rings and then.)

MAN'S VOICE: Lennox Press—Maxwell.

SOPHIE: Sophie Brill.

MAN'S VOICE: Yes ma'am.

SOPHIE: Would you read back my lead paragraph?

MAN'S VOICE: Hang on...Here we go: "With his latest picture, 'The Lake,' Gordon Rideout scoring a triple coup as producer, director, and leading man, compels me to take back every rotten thing I ever wrote about him."

SOPHIE: Thanks.

MAN'S VOICE: We go to press in one hour.

SOPHIE: No changes—just checking. *(She hangs up.)* Well?

GORDON: I'll have that drink.

SOPHIE: Scotch, vodka or bourbon?

GORDON: Anything.

SOPHIE: *(Pours two drinks—hands him his.)* What'll we drink to?

GORDON: Holy shit!

SOPHIE: *(Glass raised.)* Prosit.

GORDON: "'The best American film in ages.'—Sophie Brill."

SOPHIE: Prosit.

GORDON: I see it on buses, television, billboards.

SOPHIE: I'm partial to dirigibles.

GORDON: You know what?

SOPHIE: You did ask for a drink.

GORDON: Cheers. *(He downs it before she can react.)* I'm going to create a new ad campaign with your review the centerpiece.

SOPHIE: Cheers.

GORDON: Given the critics who don't know what they think till you speak, I predict an avalanche.

SOPHIE: You exaggerate my influence.

GORDON: You really think so?

SOPHIE: No. Refill?

GORDON: You pour while I make a call.

SOPHIE: Ms. Sobolevsky?

GORDON: Funny.

SOPHIE: Who?

GORDON: A guy in L.A. who put his ass on the line so I could make this picture and hasn't had a decent night's sleep since.

SOPHIE: I prefer you didn't.

GORDON: If you're afraid of a leak, rest easy. In addition to everything else he's a sphinx.

SOPHIE: No calls.

GORDON: Why?

SOPHIE: Guess.

GORDON: You think I've lost interest because I want to make a phone call?

SOPHIE: Prove me wrong.

GORDON: Where did we leave off?

SOPHIE: You were about to whisk me to the bedroom.

GORDON: At which point, desperate for assurance you were being loved for yourself alone, you disclosed the review.

SOPHIE: That's not why.

GORDON: Who would have guessed it? The heart of a school girl.

SOPHIE: It was your smug assumption I would demean myself.

GORDON: As a famous authority once said, "Sell it to yourself any way you like but don't take too long."

(She slaps his face. He scoops her up, bears her off. Blackout.)

SCENE II

Time: Thirty minutes later. At rise: Sophie, robe and slippers, looking out the window through partially opened drapes.

GORDON: *(Offstage.)* I need your permission to print the review in its entirety.

SOPHIE: All right.

GORDON: *(Offstage.)* I think I need it in writing

SOPHIE: All right.

GORDON: *(Offstage.)* How about dinner tomorrow night—The Four Seasons? We'll bury the hatchet conspicuously.

SOPHIE: I'm busy.

GORDON: Lunch?

SOPHIE: I'm busy all day.

GORDON: *(Enters from the bedroom carrying his sneakers which he proceeds to don.)* I wouldn't stand by the window.

SOPHIE: You think he's still lurking out there—the bogeyman?

GORDON: Why take chances?

SOPHIE: How touching.

(He regards her.)

SOPHIE: Your concern.

GORDON: Sarcasm signaling annoyance. I'm relieved.

SOPHIE: I'm not annoyed.

GORDON: You wouldn't be human if you weren't.

SOPHIE: Indignant, incensed, irate—si. But "annoyed?" Not a bit.

GORDON: Maybe now we can deal with this thing.

SOPHIE: How do you suggest we proceed.

GORDON: By leveling with each other.

SOPHIE: Sounds fun. After you.

GORDON: Strictly off the record?

SOPHIE: Wild horses.

GORDON: Painful to relate, it's not the first time—what happened in there.

SOPHIE: What *didn't* happen more to the point.

GORDON: What I'm trying to say is don't take it personally.

SOPHIE: You, reputed to have pleasured women in New York, Chicago, and Los Angeles, plus two stewardesses in transit on a single day, are unable to perform with me and you expect indifference?

GORDON: I've been working night and day for months with those loans hanging over my head. Plus chasing the mugger and the review. I'm wiped out.

SOPHIE: The other times you failed—what was the reason?

GORDON: What's the difference?

SOPHIE: I'd find specifics reassuring.

GORDON: I don't keep records.

SOPHIE: I did hear rumor of a French starlet who found you wanting at Cannes but chalked it up to sour grapes.

GORDON: You see.

SOPHIE: It's true about the French starlet?

GORDON: Oui.

SOPHIE: I made it up. Want to level some more?

GORDON: You shouldn't have told me about the review!

SOPHIE: Confirming you were only doing it for that reason.

GORDON: That isn't what I meant.

SOPHIE: Alternate interpretation eludes…Well?

GORDON: You'll say it's bullshit.

SOPHIE: Only if it is.

GORDON: The idea of you willing to compromise yourself was stimulating.

SOPHIE: I'd heard that about you: Besides a penchant for vacuous nubiles you like subjugating intelligent women.

GORDON: Is there anything about me you *don't* know?

SOPHIE: Very little given the fascination with your activities I share with most women and my superior sources.

GORDON: And now here I am, the chance of a lifetime, and you've booted it.

SOPHIE: Not necessarily.

GORDON: Meaning?

SOPHIE: If at first you don't succeed.

GORDON: Believe me the spirit's willing but the flesh is kaput.

SOPHIE: All we have to do is turn back the clock.

GORDON: Shazzam?

SOPHIE: No magic.

GORDON: I give up.

SOPHIE: The magazine doesn't go to press for thirty minutes.

GORDON: So?…You're not suggesting?

SOPHIE: A light dawns.

GORDON: I don't believe you.

(She goes to the phone. Speaker on—dials. Several rings. Then.)

MAN'S VOICE: Lennox Press—Maxwell.

SOPHIE: Sophie Brill. I'm going to dictate a change.

MAN'S VOICE: Yes ma'am.

SOPHIE: Ready?

MAN'S VOICE: Yes ma'am.

SOPHIE: "Actor, producer, director Gordon Rideout's new film, 'The Lake,' is a disaster so total the less said the better." Read it back.

MAN'S VOICE: "Actor, producer, director Gordon Rideout's new film, 'The Lake,' is a disaster so total the less said the better."

SOPHIE: How long to press?

MAN'S VOICE: Twenty-five minutes.

SOPHIE: If you don't hear from me by then run that in place of the other and use one of the standbys to fill the space. *(She hangs up before the man can reply.)* Shazzam.

GORDON: That's supposed to arouse me?

SOPHIE: Twenty-five minutes and counting.

GORDON: Not that I believe you're serious, but if that ever ran, you'd be laughed out of the business.

SOPHIE: Because everyone else is going to think your picture is so wonderful?

GORDON: Plus I'd sue your ass—subpoena the guy at the press and the original review.

SOPHIE: Since when is changing your mind a crime?

GORDON: How would you like to see me on the *Tonight* show relating all this?

SOPHIE: Including how you staged the whole thing?

GORDON: What?

SOPHIE: You know what gave it away? That fellow's oozing eye. Too grotesque, as though someone leaned on the makeup man.

GORDON: What are you talking about?

SOPHIE: Boy meets girl via faked rescue—a movie staple.

GORDON: *(Facetiously.)* And I thought I was being so original.

SOPHIE: You're wasting valuable time.

GORDON: Which might be otherwise spent?

SOPHIE: The original offer stands.

GORDON: The clock turned back?

SOPHIE: And ticking.

GORDON: I like it. How much time left?

SOPHIE: Twenty-two minutes plus an extension if things look promising.

GORDON: The extension won't be necessary. *(He embraces her.)*

SOPHIE: *(Increasingly responsive.)* You admit the whole thing was staged?

GORDON: At this moment I'd plead guilty to anything.

> *(She breaks away.)*

GORDON: Now what?

SOPHIE: How dare you patronize me.

GORDON: That wasn't my intention.

SOPHIE: Admit you hired that goon.

GORDON: You're kidding.

SOPHIE: Did you really expect me to fall for it?

GORDON: You're not kidding.

SOPHIE: How ever much you paid that creep he deserves a bonus as my increasingly sore neck will testify.

GORDON: Hold it.

SOPHIE: The cheap cologne was good but the ski mask smacked of that tendency to excess in even your latest film.

GORDON: *Shut up and listen!*...As God is my judge, I had no hand in what happened. The mugging was real.

SOPHIE: I don't believe you! *(Opening the drapes she twirls conspicuously.)* See? *(Pulling her away from the window, he closes the drapes.)*

SOPHIE: Saved again.

GORDON: You win.

SOPHIE: Meaning you admit it?

GORDON: Meaning thanks for a memorable evening.

SOPHIE: You judge me un-beddable.

GORDON: I judge myself unequal to the occasion.

SOPHIE: I thought you'd welcome challenge.

GORDON: Goodnight. *(He starts for the door.)*

SOPHIE: If I don't phone they'll run that review.

GORDON: Ruin your reputation to get at me? I don't think so. *(About to exit he looks back at her.)* I don't suppose there's any point urging again you notify the police.

SOPHIE: If I do, will you reconsider?

GORDON: Like your Danish freighter, that ship has sailed. But I'll always wonder what might have been.

(He leaves. She rushes to the door shouts after him.)

SOPHIE: You have fifteen minutes—don't cut it too close.

(We hear his steps descend—the downstairs door open and close as he leaves the building. She dashes to the window. Spots him.)

SOPHIE: Aware she's watching, he walks as though he hadn't a care…Pauses to tie a shoelace…Resumes walking…Nears the corner where… *(She turns abruptly from the window.)* If she didn't know there was a phone booth around that corner she would despair… *(Regarding the phone anxiously—expectantly.)* What will he say he left behind that he'd like to return for? His wallet? His keys?

(Phone rings.)

SOPHIE: Should she be magnanimous or make him sweat a bit?

(Rings again. She picks up.)

SOPHIE: Yes?

MAN'S VOICE: It's Maxwell. I want to be sure which review to run…Did you hear me?

SOPHIE: Yes.

MAN'S VOICE: Well?

SOPHIE: Run the first one—the original.

MAN'S VOICE: Thanks. Good night.

(We hear Maxwell hang up. Sophie does the same, goes to the liquor. As she pours a stiff shot she spots the mugger's ski mask. Puts it on. Lights down till only her head and neck are illuminated. Now her hands, as though someone else's, enter the lighted area and fasten about her throat; hold a moment. Then exert sudden pressure. Lights out.)

THE END

MATCH POINT

INTRODUCTION

It's the perfect murder in seven or eight minutes. 'Nuff said.

ORIGINAL PRODUCTION

Match Point was presented at the Ensemble Studio Theatre Marathon in 1990. The play was directed by Billy Hopkins with the following cast:

Mrs. Dunn...................... Anna Levine Thomson
Mrs. Albert .... Leslie Lyles
Mr. Albert .... W. H. Macy

SCENE I

Time: The present, noon. Place: A desert resort. Poolside, outdoors. At rise: Mrs. Albert, fortyish, bathing suit, in a lounge chair, an empty chair beside her. Mrs. Dunn, tennis attire, more attractive and several years younger than Mrs. Albert, appears. Both women wear sunglasses.

MRS. DUNN: Pardon me.

MRS. ALBERT: Yes?

MRS. DUNN: *(Indicating vacant chair.)* Are you expecting someone?

MRS. ALBERT: No.

MRS. DUNN: May I?

MRS. ALBERT: By all means.

MRS. DUNN: *(Sits: applies sun lotion to herself.)* Better make the most of it while we can.

(Mrs. Albert regards her questioningly.)

MRS. DUNN: The sun. They're talking rain next week.

MRS. ALBERT: I hadn't heard.

MRS. DUNN: A low front moving in from Canada. Or is it a high?

MRS. ALBERT: Low means bad weather. High is good.

MRS. DUNN: …First time here?

MRS. ALBERT: Gracious no. You?

MRS. DUNN: Our seventh year.

MRS. ALBERT: Our ninth.

MRS. DUNN: Every year I say to Ralph, my husband, "I love the Oasis Inn and I love the desert but please can't we take one vacation some place else?"

MRS. ALBERT: The same with Paul, my husband, and me.

MRS. DUNN: And here we are again…We're from San Francisco.

MRS. ALBERT: We're from Boston.

MRS. DUNN: *(Offering her hand.)* Grace Dunn.

MRS. ALBERT: *(Taking her hand.)* Rachel Albert.

MRS. DUNN: What time of the year do you usually come here?

MRS. ALBERT: Now.

MRS. DUNN: Now?

MRS. ALBERT: The first two weeks in March. How about you?

MRS. DUNN: The first two weeks in March.

MRS. ALBERT: No.

MRS. DUNN: Yes.

(Simultaneously they remove their sunglasses, react.)

MRS. ALBERT: Of course. I've often seen you.

MRS. DUNN: The same here.

MRS. ALBERT: All these years and we've never spoken.

MRS. DUNN: It's a large place.

MRS. ALBERT: So many people and activities.

MRS. DUNN: But no forced mingling which many resorts consider a virtue.

MRS. ALBERT: Actually it was the privacy, everyone more or less keeping to themselves, that first appealed to Paul and me.

MRS. DUNN: Ralph and I are the same. I hope I'm not intruding.

MRS. ALBERT: I hardly think a chat after so many years constitutes intrusion.

MRS. DUNN: We arrived Friday. How about you?

MRS. ALBERT: Thursday.

MRS. DUNN: Three days gone and I feel like we just got here.

MRS. ALBERT: I feel the same.

MRS. DUNN: If I'm not mistaken your husband is quite a tennis player.

MRS. ALBERT: Fanatic. Do you play?

MRS. DUNN: A bit. You?

MRS. ALBERT: No.

MRS. DUNN: …Boston?

MRS. ALBERT: Yes.

MRS. DUNN: Ralph goes to Boston occasionally on business but I've never been there.

MRS. ALBERT: We've never been to Los Angeles.

MRS. DUNN: Los Angeles?

MRS. ALBERT: Isn't that where you said you're from?

MRS. DUNN: San Francisco.

MRS. ALBERT: We've never been there either.

MRS. DUNN: …Ralph loves to fish. That's where he is now. Out on the lake. I'm not sure it's the fishing or the absence of phones so no one can reach him. He's a hospital administrator. What about your husband?

MRS. ALBERT: Stock broker.

MRS. DUNN: It must be a relief for him too. No phones except the one in the lobby.

MRS. ALBERT: Yes.

MRS. DUNN: I figure if someone wants to reach you bad enough, an emergency, they'll find a way.

MRS. ALBERT: Yes.

MRS. DUNN: …Didn't he win last year—your husband?

(Mrs. Albert regards her blankly.)

MRS. DUNN: The singles title—tennis?

MRS. ALBERT: Yes.

MRS. DUNN: Is he going to try again this year?

MRS. ALBERT: No.

MRS. DUNN: From the way a couple of the new guests play, I don't blame him. They say one fellow used to be a professional which doesn't seem fair.

MRS. ALBERT: Paul would have loved the chance to compete with a professional.

MRS. DUNN: Then why isn't he playing?

MRS. ALBERT: He isn't here.

MRS. DUNN: You're alone?

MRS. ALBERT: Yes.

MRS. DUNN: I know how that is. Several years ago Ralph had a strike to deal with and couldn't get away. I didn't want to come here without him but he insisted.

MRS. ALBERT: I think I've had enough sun. It's been nice talking to you.

MRS. DUNN: I hope your husband manages to get here for a few days. If he does, maybe you'll join us for a drink.

MRS. ALBERT: There's nothing I'd like more. But it isn't possible.

MRS. DUNN: He won't be here at all?

MRS. ALBERT: No.

MRS. DUNN: Why? I'm sorry. I shouldn't pry but you look so troubled.

MRS. ALBERT: He's dead.

MRS. DUNN: What?

MRS. ALBERT: Paul was killed in an accident three months ago.

MRS. DUNN: Oh my God.

MRS. ALBERT: I never meant to tell anyone.
   (Mrs. Dunn is frozen—traumatized.)

MRS. ALBERT: I'm sorry. Are you all right?

MRS. DUNN: Yes.

MRS. ALBERT: Can I get you something?

MRS. DUNN: An accident?

MRS. ALBERT: Yes. Death was instantaneous. I never thought I'd be able to say that without bursting into hysterics. So maybe Doctor Polan, who suggested I come here as a form of catharsis, was right: "Face your ghosts in their favorite haunts," he advised. And this place, the two weeks here every year, was certainly Paul's idea of heaven. If the invitation to have a drink with you and your husband is still in effect, I'd be pleased to join you whenever you like. Thanks ever so much. *(She goes off.)*
   (Mrs. Dunn clasps her knees, bends head to chest in fetal curl.)

SCENE II

Time: Three days later, noon. At rise: The same place. Mrs. Albert in a different bathing suit, reading a newspaper. A man in a business suit, carrying a briefcase, which marks him just arrived from the city, sneaks up behind her, puts his hands over her eyes.

MR. ALBERT: Guess who?

MRS. ALBERT: Carlos?

MR. ALBERT: No.

MRS. ALBERT: Pierre?

MR. ALBERT: No.

MRS. ALBERT: I give up.

MR. ALBERT: Who do you love most in the world?

MRS. ALBERT: My husband but he isn't due till this evening.

MR. ALBERT: I got an earlier plane. *(Mr. Albert kisses her.)*

MRS. ALBERT: From your jaunty demeanor, I'd say the merger has been achieved.

MR. ALBERT: Beyond my fondest expectations or wildest dreams. Miss me?

MRS. ALBERT: Yes.

MR. ALBERT: Besides Carlos and Pierre, what have you been doing?

MRS. ALBERT: Lounging and loafing.

MR. ALBERT: How's the weather been?

MRS. ALBERT: Ideal. How's the city?

MR. ALBERT: Less than ideal. *(Gazing about.)* Everything looks the same.

MRS. ALBERT: There's a new desk clerk. The Van Gogh print in our room has been replaced by an ugly original. The orange juice is less than freshly squeezed. Outside of that everything is exactly as we left it a year ago. Why don't you take a swim?

MR. ALBERT: After a bit of tennis to unwind. Got the room key?

MRS. ALBERT: Yes. *(As she searches her bag.)* One bit of news.

MR. ALBERT: What's that?

MRS. ALBERT: Remember that couple who come here the same weeks we do?

MR. ALBERT: No.

MRS. ALBERT: We've never spoken to them except to say hello. The husband fishes. The wife plays tennis.

MR. ALBERT: What about them?

MRS. ALBERT: Do you know who I'm talking about?

MR. ALBERT: He's short—on the round side.

MRS. ALBERT: And she's a looker. One of those couples you wonder how they got together.

MR. ALBERT: What about them?

MRS. ALBERT: You do know who I mean?

MR. ALBERT: Yes.

MRS. ALBERT: Voilà the room key. *(She dangles it.)*

MR. ALBERT: What about the Dunns?

MRS. ALBERT: The Dunns—that's right. I'm surprised.

MR. ALBERT: Surprised?

MRS. ALBERT: You usually have such trouble with names. But of course I'm forgetting—you've probably played tennis with her.

MR. ALBERT: No.

MRS. ALBERT: She hung around the courts all the time.

MR. ALBERT: I've never played with her. You said there was news. What is it?

MRS. ALBERT: She's dead.

MR. ALBERT: What?

MRS. ALBERT: Mrs. Dunn is dead.

MR. ALBERT: What are you talking about?

MRS. ALBERT: Mrs. Dunn passed away two nights ago.

MR. ALBERT: Here? She died here?

MRS. ALBERT: Yes.

MR. ALBERT: How?

MRS. ALBERT: An overdose of sleeping pills and alcohol. No note but the police suspect suicide.

MR. ALBERT: I don't believe it.

MRS. ALBERT: Why not?

MR. ALBERT: She wasn't—she didn't seem the type.

MRS. ALBERT: That's what her husband said. The management tried to keep it quiet but word leaked out. I can't tell you how shook up everyone was.

MR. ALBERT: Nobody looks very shook up now.

MRS. ALBERT: Life goes on and it wasn't as though anyone knew her very well.

MR. ALBERT: I still don't believe it.

MRS. ALBERT: It's in the weekly paper. Discreetly placed but all the pertinent information. See for yourself.

(She hands him the paper she was reading which he seizes greedily.)

MRS. ALBERT: I've got a surprise for you.

(He reads on, deaf to her words.)

MRS. ALBERT: I've started to take tennis lessons.

(He reads.)

MRS. ALBERT: I figure if tennis means that much to you, the least I can do is learn. Had my first lesson yesterday and was told by the pro that I have natural talent coupled with a killer instinct.

(He reads.)

MRS. ALBERT: Paul are you listening to me?…Paul…Paul?

THE END

A WAY WITH WORDS

INTRODUCTION

Once a year, for many years, I would meet a dear boyhood friend (now deceased) for lunch, even though we'd drifted apart and never saw each other except for these annual reunions.

Every year I'd ask how his wife, not seen nor met in ages, was. He'd say fine and we'd pass on to happy reminiscences of youthful days.

At what proved our final lunch, all went as usual till I asked after his wife and he said they'd broken up.

"When?" I asked.

"Thirteen years ago," he announced.

The playwright took it from there.

ORIGINAL PRODUCTION

A Way with Words was presented at the Ensemble Studio Theatre Marathon in 1991. The play was directed by Chris Smith.

Louise . . . . Melinda Mullins
Fred . . . . David Rasche
Artie . . . . William Wise

SCENE I

Time: Present, mid-day. Place: A corner table in a Manhattan restaurant. At rise: Artie and Fred, early forties, drinks in hand.

FRED: *I don't believe it. I do not fucking believe it.*

ARTIE: I'm sorry.

FRED: Spare me.

ARTIE: I had no idea you'd take it like this.

FRED: What did you expect?

ARTIE: You look like I hit you.

FRED: That's how I feel.

ARTIE: I should have told you when it happened.

FRED: What stopped you?

ARTIE: I figured once she had her fling she'd come back. Why make waves.

FRED: And later? When you knew it wasn't a fling?

ARTIE: I was embarrassed.

FRED: So you kept lying.

ARTIE: I never thought of it as lying.

FRED: Every year I come to New York and we have lunch and I always ask how Louise is and you always say "fine"…

ARTIE: Which she is.

FRED: …Until today when you announce that you and she aren't together any more…

ARTIE: It makes you feel better—I lied.

FRED: …"That's too bad," I say. "When did it happen?" And you say. *(Motions Artie to speak.)* Say it.

ARTIE: I said it.

FRED: Say it again so I'm sure I heard right.

ARTIE: "Louise left me thirteen years ago."

FRED: Thirteen?

ARTIE: Thirteen.

FRED: I still don't believe it.

ARTIE: Nineteen seventy-eight.

FRED: Artie if this is a joke—

ARTIE: —It's on me.

FRED: How could you not tell me?

ARTIE: We see each other once a year.

FRED: You lied because it was easy?

ARTIE: We always talk about when we were kids. Good times. I didn't want to spoil it.

FRED: Bullshit.

ARTIE: You're right.

FRED: Why then?

ARTIE: Promise not to laugh.

FRED: Artie—please.

ARTIE: Because you thought she and I were still together made it seem true for a few hours.

FRED: Jesus.

ARTIE: Sometimes after our lunches I was so into it I expected to find her there when I got home.

FRED: Thirteen years and you're still carrying a torch?

ARTIE: Never changed the lock on the door or the phone number in case she—

FRED: —I get the picture. The Christmas cards with both your signatures?

ARTIE: Forged.

FRED: And that's why whenever I phoned I got you.

ARTIE: You didn't phone that often.

FRED: The phone works both ways.

ARTIE: You can only talk so much about boyhood memories.

FRED: We went separate ways—okay. But I always felt I could rely on you in an emergency.

ARTIE: I feel the same.

FRED: Your wife walking out wasn't an emergency?

ARTIE: What could you have done?

FRED: Provided a sympathetic ear at least.

ARTIE: I felt sorry enough for myself without encouragement.

FRED: Why did she do it?

ARTIE: I guess she wasn't happy.

FRED: You guess?

ARTIE: I come home from work. She's at the door, bags packed, cab waiting. Hands me a list of household things that need doing. Says it will be best for both of us in the long run. The next thing I know the cab is turning the corner and I'm waving with a smile on my face like she's going to visit her mother in case any neighbors are watching.

FRED: There must have been warning signs.

ARTIE: If so I missed them.

FRED: "It will be best for both of us in the long run?"

ARTIE: Verbatim.

FRED: That's all she said?

ARTIE: From that day to this.

FRED: What's become of her?

ARTIE: Remarried. Has two kids. Maybe if we'd had kids.

FRED: Who's the guy?

ARTIE: Someone she met later. A lawyer. They live on Central Park West. A duplex. Plus a house in Connecticut. The boy's ten—the girl's seven. The dog's name is Skippy.

FRED: You keep in touch.

ARTIE: No.

FRED: Well how do you know all this?

ARTIE: She stayed friends with a cousin of mine.

FRED: What about *you?*

ARTIE: What about me?

FRED: Any women in your life?

ARTIE: Women—yes. Woman—close but no cigar.

FRED: You live alone.

ARTIE: Essentially. How's *your* family?

FRED: Fine.

ARTIE: Your youngest son was going to have a disc operation.

FRED: He's a hundred percent.

ARTIE: And your eldest?

FRED: I don't want to talk about them.

ARTIE: You're still upset.

FRED: Wouldn't you be if I said "Oh by the way, Ann and I split up thirteen years ago?"

ARTIE: No.

FRED: You wouldn't care?

ARTIE: I'd care but it's not the same. I never met Ann. You know Louise as long as I do—you were our best man.

FRED: Which you were supposed to be at *my* wedding until…Hold the phone.

ARTIE: A light dawns.

FRED: Louise left in seventy-eight?

ARTIE: April twelfth. A day that shall live in infamy.

FRED: I got married that May.

ARTIE: You're getting warm.

FRED: That's why you canceled.

ARTIE: Head of the class.

FRED: The story about your mother too sick for you and Louise to come to California—

ARTIE: —The first of many deceptions.

FRED: Why did I never catch on?

ARTIE: I often wondered.

FRED: Implying I let you down somehow?

ARTIE: Not at all.

FRED: What then?

ARTIE: Some of the excuses I invented why Louise never joined us for lunch or why we didn't invite you to the house were pretty wild.

FRED: It's easy to fool people who trust you.

ARTIE: Maybe I missed my calling.

FRED: Meaning?

ARTIE: Maybe *I* should have become the writer and *you* should be the accountant.

FRED: Judging by the reviews of my last book you're not alone in that opinion.

ARTIE: I'm half-way through it.

FRED: Since it's been out eight months I gather that's a criticism.

ARTIE: I got bogged down in the long flashback.

FRED: Would you mind sticking to the subject at hand?

ARTIE: You're not interested in my opinion?

FRED: Not today. And *why* today after thirteen years?

ARTIE: You said you felt you could count on me in an emergency and I said the feeling was mutual.

FRED: What about it?

ARTIE: I've been seeing this woman and the time has come to legalize our relationship or end it. She's attractive, wealthy, got a good sense of humor and adores me.

FRED: But?

ARTIE: I've still got this thing for Louise.

FRED: That's ridiculous.

ARTIE: I'm not interested in your advice or opinion.

FRED: What then?

ARTIE: My cousin said Louise and her husband haven't been getting along.

FRED: Which you read as a favorable sign?

ARTIE: It's possible.

FRED: Talk about clutching straws.

ARTIE: I want to be sure it's over before I marry this other woman.

FRED: Artie take my word.

ARTIE: I want you to speak to Louise.

FRED: What?

ARTIE: I want you to sound her out and tell me if you think it's hopeless.

FRED: You can't be serious.

ARTIE: You said I could count on you in an emergency.

FRED: Emergency yes. This is craziness.

ARTIE: You won't do it.

FRED: If I saw any point I'd be glad to.

(Artie rises taking money from his wallet and throwing it on the table.)

FRED: What are you doing?

ARTIE: It's my year to pay.

FRED: We haven't eaten.

ARTIE: I lost my appetite.

FRED: Sit down.

ARTIE: Next time you're in town—don't call.

(He would leave but Fred grabs his arm.)

FRED: Sit down God damn it.

ARTIE: What's the point?

FRED: Artie, we know each other longer than anybody else in our lives.

ARTIE: And the first time I ask a favor you turn me down.

FRED: I didn't turn you down.

ARTIE: You said it was crazy.

FRED: It *is* crazy.

ARTIE: But you'll do it?

FRED: I haven't seen or spoken to Louise in thirteen years. Do I phone? Knock at the door? Suppose her husband answers? Think about it.

ARTIE: *(Resuming his seat.)* I have. And I've got it all worked out. Want to hear?

FRED: No. *(Hastily as Artie reacts.)* But I will.

ARTIE: Every day, weather permitting, she jogs in Central Park from one to two o'clock.

FRED: Let me guess: I accidentally bump into her.

ARTIE: Right.

FRED: Then what?

ARTIE: You steer the conversation around to whether she has any regrets about leaving me.

FRED: Assuming there *is* a conversation.

ARTIE: Why wouldn't there be?

FRED: I never contacted her. She might be pissed.

ARTIE: Did *she* ever contact *you?*

FRED: No.

ARTIE: So you're even.

FRED: Why don't *you* "bump" into her and find out first hand?

ARTIE: I tried.

FRED: You spoke to her?

ARTIE: I went to the park last week with every intention of doing so. Spotted her and got so choked up I couldn't go through with it.

FRED: It's not going to work Artie. I'll do it if you insist but it's a mistake.

ARTIE: I insist.

FRED: Okay. But no "accidental" meeting. I'll tell her I just learned about the breakup and—

ARTIE: —*No way.*

FRED: Why not?

ARTIE: She thinks you've known from the beginning.

FRED: You told her you told me?

ARTIE: Yes.

FRED: Why?

ARTIE: I figured if I didn't *she'd* tell you and the more people who knew the less chance of our getting back together.

FRED: If I knew, why didn't I get in touch with her? What must she think?

ARTIE: That you blame her for what happened.

FRED: Why would she think that?

ARTIE: Because that's what I said.

FRED: You told her I blamed her for leaving you?

ARTIE: I thought it might carry some weight.

FRED: You know what I feel like doing right now?

ARTIE: You wanna poke me go ahead.

FRED: Where the hell do you come off—

ARTIE: —I was out of my mind.

FRED: I'm lucky she doesn't slug me.

ARTIE: I guarantee she'll be glad to see you.

FRED: On the basis of what?

ARTIE: If she was mad at you, would she buy your books?

FRED: She does?

ARTIE: My cousin says she has every book and story you ever published plus copies of interviews. *(Eyes his watch.)* She should reach the reservoir in about ten minutes.

FRED: I bump into her by accident. "Is that who I think it is?" "It can't be." Then what?

ARTIE: You'll think of something.

FRED: How will I recognize her?

ARTIE: She'll be wearing a yellow or green jogging suit and a Mets baseball cap. Plus she hasn't changed.

FRED: The reservoir?

ARTIE: Yes.

FRED: *(Rising.)* Here goes nothing.

ARTIE: I appreciate what you're doing.

FRED: Thanks.

ARTIE: I mean it.

FRED: Save it till you see what happens.

ARTIE: Whatever happens don't let on I put you up to it, or that you haven't known about the breakup from the beginning.

FRED: My lips are sealed on one condition.

ARTIE: Which is?

FRED: If I come back and say your chances with Louise are zero, will you marry that woman?

ARTIE: Deal.

FRED: You mean it?

ARTIE: My mother's head.

FRED: Yellow or green?

ARTIE: And a Mets cap.

(Fred goes off. Artie sipping his drink looks after him.)

SCENE II

Time: Thirty minutes later. Place: A bench in Central Park. At rise: Louise, late thirties to early forties, well preserved, vivacious, in a green jogging suit and Mets cap, shares the bench with Fred.

LOUISE: If I'm staring like an idiot, it's because that's how I feel.

FRED: Same here.

LOUISE: I'm staggered.

FRED: Likewise.

LOUISE: It's really you.

FRED: As far as I know.

LOUISE: I don't believe it.

FRED: That makes two of us.

LOUISE: I knew our paths would cross. But Central Park? Me like this? How did you recognize me?

FRED: You haven't changed.

LOUISE: Why didn't *I* recognize *you?*

FRED: You were jogging.

LOUISE: I mean after you stopped me. I'm thinking I know this guy but who is he?

FRED: I haven't aged as gracefully as you.

LOUISE: You do look older.

FRED: Thanks.

LOUISE: Why shouldn't you? It's been thirteen years. *(She removes the Mets cap—frees her hair, which she points to.)* Look close—lots of gray. Feel better? The farewell party.

FRED: What?

LOUISE: The party when you moved to California. That's the last time we met.

FRED: You sure?

LOUISE: Positive. We spoke on the phone when you said you were getting married and asked Artie to be your best man. But the last time we saw each other was the going away party.

FRED: The only thing I remember about that party was a monumental hangover.

LOUISE: The Castle Grill on Route Seventeen. You thought you were going to a business meeting.

FRED: I remember getting there and being surprised. Everything after that is a blank.

LOUISE: So here we are.

FRED: At long last.

LOUISE: Too long.

FRED: Much.

LOUISE: He called you right away.

FRED: What?

LOUISE: When I left, Artie said the first thing he did was phone you.

FRED: Yes.

LOUISE: You must have been jolted.

FRED: Yes.

LOUISE: Did he say why I left him.

FRED: He had no idea.

LOUISE: Subtext was never Artie's strong suit.

FRED: He said the only reason you gave was that it would be best for both of you in the long run.

LOUISE: What a bitch I was—huh?

FRED: I wouldn't say that.

LOUISE: You *did* say it.

FRED: Artie said I called you a bitch?

LOUISE: Among other less flattering things. Which is probably why I didn't recognize you. You don't expect a person who hates you to hail you with a smile on their face.

FRED: I never hated you.

LOUISE: Artie said you said—

FRED: —No matter what Artie said, I never hated you.

LOUISE: Then why didn't you call me?

FRED: Because… *(About to level, he recalls his promise to Artie.)* I'm not sure.

LOUISE: Face it, you were angry. I'd "betrayed" your best friend.

FRED: Maybe I was a bit sore.

LOUISE: More than a bit or you'd have contacted me.

FRED: I was furious—okay?

LOUISE: "Was" meaning you're not any more?

FRED: Yes.

LOUISE: When did you stop?

FRED: Years ago.

LOUISE: Why didn't you get in touch with me then?

FRED: Too much time had passed. What could I say?

LOUISE: For openers you might have apologized for bum rapping me.

FRED: I apologize.

LOUISE: Too little—too late. But thanks anyway.

FRED: Why didn't *you* call *me?*

LOUISE: So you could repeat the awful things you said personally?

FRED: Given your side of the story I might have felt differently.

LOUISE: There was only one side at that point.

FRED: What do you mean?

LOUISE: I shared the general opinion that in deserting such a decent, loyal, loving, hard-working man, I'd done a sinful thing.

FRED: You don't feel that way any more.

LOUISE: Not for ages. How's Ann?

FRED: Ann?

LOUISE: Your wife. Isn't that her name?

FRED: She's fine.

LOUISE: Tim and Eric?

FRED: Also fine.

LOUISE: They look fine.

(His expression asks how she knows.)

LOUISE: The jacket photos on your books.

FRED: You read my stuff?

LOUISE: Every word.

FRED: I'm flattered.

LOUISE: I didn't say I liked it.

FRED: Ouch.

LOUISE: Would you want me to lie?

FRED: Yes.

LOUISE: Actually I like most of your work a lot.

FRED: Thanks.

LOUISE: But not the last book.

FRED: The flashback sucks.

LOUISE: In a word. Would you mind if I touched you?

FRED: *(Offering his hand.)* Be my guest.

LOUISE: *(Touches him playfully.)* I'm beginning to think this is really happening.

FRED: And I'm starting to feel it's a dream.

LOUISE: How's Artie?

FRED: How should I know?

LOUISE: A cousin of his I'm friends with said you see him when you come to New York.

FRED: Not always.

LOUISE: You haven't seen him this trip.

FRED: No.

LOUISE: Are you going to?

FRED: Maybe.

LOUISE: I hope so.

FRED: Why?

LOUISE: His cousin said your visits mean a lot to him.

FRED: You keep tabs on him?

LOUISE: Just what his cousin tells me.

FRED: Do you ever regret leaving him?

LOUISE: Are you kidding?

FRED: I thought maybe—

LOUISE: —Artie is a sweet guy who might have had a happy life if he hadn't met me. I feel bad about that but that's all I feel.

FRED: You really have your act together.

LOUISE: Three and a half years on the couch—I should. Ever indulge?

FRED: Analysis?

LOUISE: Yes.

FRED: No.

LOUISE: You never felt the need or because you feared tampering with the creative process?

FRED: The latter mostly.

LOUISE: Nature abhors a vacuum.

FRED: So they say.

LOUISE: You get rid of old preoccupations new thoughts take their place.

FRED: Thus spake Sigmund.

LOUISE: Via Doctor Millstein.

FRED: In short, as a writer, I'm repeating myself?

LOUISE: Yes.

FRED: What about the science stuff in the last book?

LOUISE: Mere background for your usual concerns.

FRED: Serves me right for picking up a girl in Central Park.

LOUISE: It's only my opinion.

FRED: You left out "humble."

LOUISE: I don't feel humble.

FRED: Maybe you should give me Doctor Millstein's phone number.

LOUISE: If you like.

FRED: What I'd like is no more literary discussion.

LOUISE: In favor of what?

FRED: It's been thirteen years—fill me in.

LOUISE: What would you like to know?

FRED: You said you thought it would be best for both of you.

LOUISE: I was half right.

FRED: You're happy. Artie's not.

LOUISE: Right.

FRED: Why?

LOUISE: Why am I happy or why has he become keeper of the eternal flame?

FRED: You don't sound very sympathetic.

LOUISE: I married him knowing I didn't love him. Shame on me. He keeps a candle in the window for thirteen years. More fool he.

FRED: You never loved him?

LOUISE: Never.

FRED: Not even in the beginning when we used to double date?

LOUISE: Not even then.

FRED: You sure fooled me.

LOUISE: Not half as much as I fooled myself.

FRED: Artie said your husband's a lawyer—you have two kids.

LOUISE: Does he still think things might have worked out different if *we'd* had kids?

FRED: He mentioned the possibility.

LOUISE: God what a horse's ass! I'm sorry. It's just that I've been hearing this pathetic crap from the day I walked out. How he's never changed the door locks or the phone number.

FRED: His cousin keeps you posted.

LOUISE: In painful detail.

FRED: Did she tell you he's seeing someone and it's serious?

LOUISE: Yes. And once again I have my fingers crossed.

FRED: You'd like him to remarry.

LOUISE: More than anything.

FRED: The only thing stopping him is the hope that somehow, some day you'll go back to him.

LOUISE: What else is new?

FRED: I'm going to tell him I bumped into you and we had a long chat during which I realized there's no way on earth you'll ever return.

LOUISE: Lots of luck.

FRED: I'll tell him your marriage couldn't be better.

LOUISE: Which is so.

FRED: I can see that and I'm glad for you.

LOUISE: If he needs more proof tell him I'm pregnant.

FRED: Really?

LOUISE: Three months.

FRED: Doesn't show.

LOUISE: Want to feel?

FRED: I'll take your word. Congratulations.

LOUISE: Thanks. *(Regards her watch.)* I've got to pick my daughter up at school. Want to come along?

FRED: I'd love to but I've got an appointment.

(Both rise.)

LOUISE: I'm glad we met.

FRED: So am I. *(Offering his hand.)* Goodbye.

LOUISE: A far cry from our last parting.

FRED: What?

LOUISE: The farewell party. Artie went to get the car while you and I waited by the entrance...

FRED: And?

LOUISE: You kissed me...No memory at all?

FRED: No.

LOUISE: Suppose I told you I took that kiss to mean that you were moving to California because you felt distance was the only way to insure that you wouldn't make a play for your best friend's wife whom you secretly adored?

FRED: That must have been some kiss.

LOUISE: It started long before that.

FRED: It?

LOUISE: The crush I had on you.

FRED: You never let on.

LOUISE: You guys were pals. Plus I never detected the slightest interest on your part until that kiss when I convinced myself the feeling was mutual.

FRED: Why are you telling me this?

LOUISE: They say confession is good for the soul.

FRED: Feel better?

LOUISE: I'm not through. That kiss changed my life.

FRED: What?

LOUISE: When you called from California to say you were getting married I read it as an ultimatum to leave Artie or forever hold my peace.

FRED: Are you saying—

LOUISE: —Yes. I left him confident you'd contact me as soon as you heard. And we'd live happily ever after. But you didn't call. And as the date of your wedding neared I grew desperate. Called Artie on some pretext to be sure you knew we'd split. He said he told you right after I left and you pronounced me a bitch, et cetera.

FRED: I never said that!

LOUISE: What you said doesn't matter. The point is you didn't get in touch with me and I began to realize I'd been deluding myself. Went into a depression compounded by alcohol that saw me hospitalized the day after your wedding. Enter Doctor Millstein.

FRED: I can't tell you how bad I feel.

LOUISE: Why? If not for that kiss I might have stayed with Artie—missed out on the wonderful life I now enjoy. To quote the good doctor—I owe you.

FRED: Glad to have been of service.

LOUISE: If you mean that there's one more thing you can do.

FRED: What is it?

LOUISE: Kiss me goodbye.

(He initiates a brief and tentative embrace.)

LOUISE: I meant like you did that night at the party.

FRED: I don't remember what I did.

LOUISE: It was something like this.

(She cups his face in her hands and presses her lips to his in a kiss that is tender, passionate and probing. He, arms at his sides, the passive recipient at first. Then his arms slowly rise and he is about to enfold her when she breaks off.)

LOUISE: Ring any bells?

FRED: No. Sorry.

LOUISE: What's to be sorry?

FRED: That I don't remember something that means so much to you.

LOUISE: Not "means"—meant.

FRED: (Lightly.) It's over between us?

LOUISE: And has been for years. The kiss was to make sure. Ciao.

(She goes off. He stands there.)

SCENE III

Time: Fifteen minutes later. Place: Same as Scene I. At rise: Fred and Artie as before.

ARTIE: And?

FRED: And what?

ARTIE: What else did she say?

FRED: That's it.

ARTIE: You were gone close to an hour.

FRED: It took most of that time to find her.

ARTIE: She was surprised.

FRED: Yes.

ARTIE: What did she say?

FRED: I told you.

ARTIE: I mean when you stopped her. What were her first words?

FRED: What difference does it make?

ARTIE: I'd like to know.

FRED: Why?

ARTIE: Maybe you missed something.

FRED: Artie look. She's never coming back to you. That's the bottom line.

ARTIE: *Fuck the bottom line! (Hastily apologetic.)* I'm sorry. Just tell me everything so I can be sure. Please.

FRED: She and her husband are getting along fine.

ARTIE: She said that?

FRED: Yes.

ARTIE: I heard different.

FRED: You heard wrong.

ARTIE: You think she's going to bump into someone she hasn't seen in thirteen years and tell them personal problems?

FRED: She's pregnant.

ARTIE: Pregnant?

FRED: Pregnant.

ARTIE: My cousin never mentioned it.

FRED: She probably doesn't know.

ARTIE: Why would Louise tell you before my cousin?

FRED: She told me to tell you she was pregnant in the hope it would kill any hopes you had about her once and for all.

ARTIE: She actually said that?

FRED: Yes.

ARTIE: Wow.

FRED: Convinced?

ARTIE: That does sound pretty final.

FRED: I'd say so.

ARTIE: How did she look?

FRED: Remarkably unchanged.

ARTIE: Green or yellow?…The jogging suit.

FRED: Green.

ARTIE: Mets cap?

FRED: Yes.

ARTIE: Pregnant?

FRED: Three months.

ARTIE: *(Overwhelmed—wipes his eyes.)* Forgive me.

FRED: No need.

ARTIE: Nice thing to lay on a guy comes to New York for a good time.

FRED: What are friends for?

ARTIE: Boyhood buddies. A secret revealed after thirteen years. Maybe you'll get a story out of it so it's not a total loss.

FRED: Maybe.

ARTIE: *(Blows his nose.)* Does she know I'm thinking about getting married?

FRED: Yes.

ARTIE: And?

FRED: She hopes you go through with it.

ARTIE: Just what I always wanted—her blessing.

FRED: You said if I told you it was thumbs down—

ARTIE: —Want to be best man again?

FRED: You're going to do it?

ARTIE: Yes.

FRED: Congratulations.

ARTIE: Thanks.

FRED: You're doing the right thing.

ARTIE: It's a done deal. Don't sell me.

FRED: Sorry.

ARTIE: What's to be sorry? Actually I feel pretty good.

FRED: I'm glad.

ARTIE: Like a big weight's been lifted. Like…Like…

FRED: A sense of new beginnings?

ARTIE: Bull's-eye. Anyone ever tell you you have a way with words?

FRED: Not recently.

ARTIE: If you get a story out of it, you'll change things so no one can point a finger.

FRED: Of course.

ARTIE: "A sense of new beginnings." That's exactly how I feel.

FRED: Suppose I loved Louise?

ARTIE: What?

FRED: Suppose I secretly loved Louise and would have told her if I'd known she left you. How's that for a switch?…Well?

ARTIE: I'm thinking. *(He ponders a moment—then definitely.)* I like it.

FRED: You don't think it's too far fetched?

ARTIE: Not for a story. I can't tell you how good I feel. You know what I'm going to do? I'm going to propose tonight. This calls for champagne! *(He beckons off.)* Waiter.

(Freeze—Artie with his hand in the air.)

THE END

GIVE THE BISHOP
MY FAINT REGARDS

INTRODUCTION

Two actors whose work I liked (names mercifully not included for reasons that will be made clear) were offered the lead roles and accepted.

I attended rehearsals (Daniel Selznick—director) until satisfied the script was locked and working.

The afternoon of opening night I received an urgent call from Selznick that, for whatever reason, the two actors had hijacked the play and transformed it into something far removed from the one I'd written.

I said I'd be there in an hour and jumped in my car.

Gorge rising with each passing mile, I braced for confrontation.

Arrived at EST ready for war, only to learn the actors had fled.

In war, an act warranting execution. In theater, inviting a complaint to Equity, which would still force us to cancel the play opening night—three hours away.

My fortune-telling grandmother always said my ultimate destiny was to be an actor.

The show would go on!

Danny Selznick, Janet Zarish (a real actor—bless her), and I gave a script-in-hand reading of the play.

How did we fare?

Let me quote from the framed copy of Mel Gussow's *New York Times* review that adorns my work room:

> With characteristic Gilroy savvy, this is a cleverly plotted picture of a team of old Hollywood hands…Mr. Gilroy and Mr. Selznick are not professional actors, but both are close enough to the play and to the Hollywood that inspired it to give a reading a certain veracity. Even without rehearsal, Ms. Zarish is on top of her catalytic role as a craft interviewer.
>
> In contrast to David Mamet's high powered *Speed the Plow,* Mr. Gilroy's play has an easygoing affability while making related satiric points. If it were appropriately cast and staged, *Give the Bishop* would be a pungent insider's report on peer and career pressures in the insanely competitive world of movies.

Danny and I held the fort until two gallant professionals (Jordan Charney and Victor Raider Wexler) joined Janet Zarish. 'Gallant' because they went on with but a day to prepare and performed admirably.

Alas, Mel Gussow never returned, so their fine work went unrecorded.

Incidentally the setting of this play is again that writers' bungalow patterned after the one I occupied at Twentieth Century Fox in 1958–1959.

As much as I enjoyed the experience, and with all due respect for my grandmother's celebrated prescience, she was wrong about my destiny as an actor.

Even as I performed, I was perceiving it from the audience side where I belonged.

As for the derelict duo, we never filed a complaint.

How could we, given the memorable and pleasureful experience they'd inadvertently provided.

ORIGINAL PRODUCTION

Give the Bishop My Faint Regards was presented at the Ensemble Studio Theatre Marathon in 1992. The play was directed by Daniel Selznick with the following cast:

Rossi. . . . . Jordan Charney
Glantz. . . . . Victor Raider-Wexler
Interviewer . . . . Janet Zarish

Time: A weekday afternoon. Place: A writer's office at a movie studio in Hollywood. At Rise: A woman, late twenties to early thirties, microcassette recorder on the table beside the chair she occupies, interviewing the screen-writing team of Rossi and Glantz—both in their fifties or sixties.

INTERVIEWER: What brought you together?

ROSSI: Hunger.

INTERVIEWER: Seriously.

GLANTZ: Seriously. I had just become a father for the second time, and he had been dispossessed for the third time.

ROSSI: Neither of us had worked in a year.

INTERVIEWER: So you decided to join forces?

GLANTZ: Decide? No. It was fate.

ROSSI: We had the same agent, but we didn't know each other.

GLANTZ: One day, we both happened to be in the agent's office when he gets a call from a producer at Metro who needs a quick rewrite.

ROSSI: But there's a catch.

GLANTZ: He wants a team—two heads for the price of one.

ROSSI: I look at *him.* He looks at *me.*

GLANTZ: The rest, as they say, is history.

INTERVIEWER: "Trouble in Tampico"—additional dialogue by Rossi and Glantz.

ROSSI: Head of the class.

GLANTZ: It would have been Glantz and Rossi but he won the toss.

INTERVIEWER: That means you've been collaborating for over twenty years.

ROSSI: Twenty-two years, three months and four days. But who's counting?

GLANTZ: *(Indicating the recorder.)* You sure that thing's getting all these pearls?

WOMAN: *(Displaying the recorder.)* Voice activated. Guaranteed to pick up anything within fifty feet.

(The phone rings. Rossi picks up.)

ROSSI: Hello. *(Covers the mouthpiece. To Glantz.)* Guess who?

GLANTZ: Vogel?

ROSSI: Vogel. *(On the phone.)* What's the good word?…Slow but sure… *(Mouthpiece covered—to Glantz.)* He wants to hear what we've got so far.

GLANTZ: When?

ROSSI: Today.

GLANTZ: No way.

ROSSI: You tell him.

GLANTZ: *(Taking the phone.)* How ya doing, boss?…We're more than half way through the outline…It's going fine but you know how we hate to present unfinished work…Yes…I understand…Right…Right. *(Hangs up.)*

ROSSI: What did he say?

GLANTZ: Three guesses.

ROSSI: Command performance.

GLANTZ: His office—six p.m.

ROSSI: *(To the interviewer.)* As you can see we're under the gun.

INTERVIEWER: Ten minutes more?

GLANTZ: Five.

INTERVIEWER: You're credited with eighteen films.

ROSSI: Twelve of which we wrote ourselves.

GLANTZ: Plus six we shared credit.

ROSSI: Plus others…

GLANTZ: …which shall be nameless…

ROSSI: …we made significant contributions but got screwed.

GLANTZ: Ask about awards.

ROSSI: One Oscar nomination.

GLANTZ: One Golden Globe.

ROSSI: One Writer's Guild award.

GLANTZ: Plus two Writer's Guild nominations.

ROSSI: And still going strong.

GLANTZ: Stronger than ever.

ROSSI: Be sure and mention that so people don't think it's an obituary.

INTERVIEWER: How do you work?

GLANTZ: Hard.

INTERVIEWER: I mean who does what?

ROSSI: I pace.

GLANTZ: I type.

INTERVIEWER: Is there a division of labor? One of you better at story, the other at dialogue?

ROSSI: No.   GLANTZ: No.

INTERVIEWER: You do everything together?

ROSSI: Absolutely.   GLANTZ: Positively.

INTERVIEWER: What happens when you disagree?

ROSSI: We don't.

INTERVIEWER: Not one difference of opinion in twenty years?

GLANTZ: Except the time I wanted to have lunch at the Brown Derby and he insisted on Scandia.

ROSSI: So we went to Nate and Al's.

GLANTZ: I had the cobb salad.

ROSSI: I had lox and eggs.

INTERVIEWER: In other words, don't ask.

ROSSI: Frankly I don't think anyone's interested how screenwriters work.

GLANTZ: Not even our families.

ROSSI: Especially our families.

GLANTZ: You want people to read this, ask about the time we had lunch with Elizabeth Taylor who played footsie with me under the table.

ROSSI: You never told me that.

GLANTZ: I didn't want to make you jealous.

ROSSI: Suppose I told you while playing footsie with you, she was doing the same thing with me.

GLANTZ: No.

ROSSI: Yes.

INTERVIEWER: "The Countess and the Thief." MGM. Two generals dining with the Countess think they're rubbing feet with her only to discover they're doing it with each other.

GLANTZ: You really did your homework.

INTERVIEWER: Yes.

ROSSI: For the record, we did have lunch with Elizabeth Taylor.

GLANTZ: Whose foot did touch his by accident.

ROSSI: Which I mentioned to him. And voilà.

GLANTZ: The scene was born.

INTERVIEWER: Would you say that was typical of the way you worked?

ROSSI: No.　　　　　　GLANTZ: Yes.

INTERVIEWER: Which is it?

ROSSI: *(Indicating Glantz.)* What *he* said.

GLANTZ: *(Indicating Rossi.)* What *he* said.

INTERVIEWER: Fellows look—I did my homework in the hope of eliciting more than gags.

GLANTZ: What did she say?

ROSSI: She wants to know what we do behind closed doors.

GLANTZ: For shame.

INTERVIEWER: I happen to believe screenwriters are the unsung heroes of the industry.

GLANTZ: On behalf of the Writer's Guild we thank you.

INTERVIEWER: Maybe if the public knew more about what you do, you might get the respect you deserve.

ROSSI: I think I'm falling in love.

GLANTZ: I think we're in the presence of a serious student of the movies.

ROSSI: I think you mean cinema.

INTERVIEWER: I feel there's a chemistry in writing teams that neither partner understands which is why you resist any probing.

GLANTZ: Your five minutes just expired.

INTERVIEWER: One more question?

ROSSI: In less than three hours we have to pitch a story to the head of the studio.

GLANTZ: A story whose through line has so far eluded us.

ROSSI: Ergo we're gonna have to blow smoke and tap dance.

GLANTZ: That's off the record you understand.

INTERVIEWER: Just one last question?

ROSSI: Shoot.

INTERVIEWER: "Give the bishop my faint regards."

ROSSI: *(Grimacing.)* Oh boy.

GLANTZ: *(To the interviewer.)* How did I know you were going to say that?

INTERVIEWER: It's one of the all time movie lines. Right up there with, "Here's looking at you kid."

ROSSI: You'd like to know which of us wrote it.

INTERVIEWER: Yes.

GLANTZ: Any idea how many times we've been asked that?

INTERVIEWER: Yes. And I know the answer: "We don't remember."

ROSSI: Which still applies.

INTERVIEWER: Since this is the first interview you've done in ages, I was hoping something might have jogged your memory.

GLANTZ: Sorry to disappoint.

INTERVIEWER: Why do I think if you did remember you wouldn't tell me?

ROSSI: We really have to get to work.

INTERVIEWER: *(She picks up the recorder; puts it in a leather tote bag.)* Thanks for your time.

GLANTZ: Sorry we can't spare more.

INTERVIEWER: *(One last try.)* If one of you had a sudden flash who wrote it would you tell the other just between yourselves?

ROSSI: No.   GLANTZ: Yes.

INTERVIEWER: Which is it?

GLANTZ: What *he* said.

ROSSI: What *he* said.

INTERVIEWER: I think this is where I came in.

GLANTZ: 'Fraid so.

(She starts to root through her tote bag.)

GLANTZ: What are you looking for?

INTERVIEWER: My card, in case you think of anything you want to add. *(As she rummages, the bag falls to the floor spilling some of its contents which she hastily retrieves, finding her card in the process.)* Here you go.

(Rossi takes the card.)

INTERVIEWER: Thanks again.

GLANTZ: Our pleasure.

INTERVIEWER: Goodbye.

ROSSI: Goodbye.

(She goes.)

ROSSI: That's the last interview we ever do.

GLANTZ: I didn't want to do it in the first place.

ROSSI: Same shit every time. Where were we?

GLANTZ: *(Sits at the desk; reads from the page in the typewriter.)* The seventh body has just been found.

ROSSI: Like it's the only thing we ever wrote.

GLANTZ: In common with the other six bodies, there are teeth marks made by something so unusual that the authorities ask for a news blackout to prevent a panic.

ROSSI: "Give the bishop my faint regards." Big deal.

GLANTZ: When you hear the signal the time will be three twenty-five.

(Rossi regards him.)

GLANTZ: Vogel expects us at six o'clock.

ROSSI: How about the authorities don't want news of the latest victim to get out. Ask for a news blackout to prevent a panic.

GLANTZ: I've got that.

ROSSI: The chief jumps all over Inspector Mooney.

GLANTZ: He did that after the sixth murder.

ROSSI: *(Mimicking the interviewer.)* "I think screenwriters are unsung heroes."

GLANTZ: *(Getting up.)* When you're ready to work, let me know.

ROSSI: What's with you?

GLANTZ: We have a lot to do.

ROSSI: Inspector Mooney spots something about the seventh victim that jogs his memory.

GLANTZ: His memory of what?

ROSSI: The woman who lived next door to the first victim.

GLANTZ: What did he spot?

ROSSI: We'll fill it in later.

GLANTZ: Vogel likes specifics.

ROSSI: We're looking for a through line.

GLANTZ: Then what?

ROSSI: We'll get to the details.

GLANTZ: I mean "then what" after Mooney recalls the woman who lived next door to the first victim.

ROSSI: He goes to interview her again only to find—

GLANTZ: —she's dead.

ROSSI: Missing.

GLANTZ: Dead is better.

ROSSI: She can't be.

GLANTZ: Why not?

ROSSI: Vogel promised the role to his current bimbo.

GLANTZ: How do you know?

ROSSI: I know.

GLANTZ: *(Resumes his seat at the desk. Types.)* Seventh victim…Something about the corpse makes Mooney think of first victim's neighbor. *(To Rossi.)* And then? *(Realizing Rossi isn't listening.)* Knock-knock.

ROSSI: We must have written a hundred thousand lines—two hundred thousand. Why should we remember that one?

GLANTZ: Like she said, it's famous.

ROSSI: Did we know it was going to be famous when we wrote it?

GLANTZ: What's wrong with you?

ROSSI: "Authors of 'Give the bishop my faint regards' pass away." That's going to be our obituary.

GLANTZ: As long as it mentions we were in our nineties en route to an orgy, who cares?

ROSSI: It doesn't bother you?

GLANTZ: Most people aren't remembered for anything.

ROSSI: How well you take it.

GLANTZ: Want me to call Vogel—say we ran into a snag?

ROSSI: No.

GLANTZ: We're not going to finish at this rate.

ROSSI: Why did you say yes?

GLANTZ: What?

ROSSI: When she asked if one of us suddenly remembered who wrote the line, would we tell each other. I said no—you said yes.

GLANTZ: So what?

ROSSI: Your answer puzzles me.

GLANTZ: I said the first thing popped in my head to get rid of her.

ROSSI: Why yes?

GLANTZ: Next time I'll say no. Okay?

ROSSI: Yes or no is all the same to you?

GLANTZ: It was a hypothetical question.

ROSSI: If I told you right now I wrote 'Give the bishop my faint regards' and could prove it, you wouldn't be upset?

GLANTZ: Not as long as we kept it to ourselves.

ROSSI: Suppose I announced it to the world?

GLANTZ: You'd never do that.

ROSSI: I'm flattered.

GLANTZ: Flattered?

ROSSI: That you think I'm so honorable.

GLANTZ: Who said honorable?

ROSSI: What then?

GLANTZ: If you went around broadcasting that the most famous line we wrote was your brainchild, it would jeopardize our relationship which I don't think you want to do.

ROSSI: Why do I feel like in junior high when Morty Berman challenged me to meet him after school?

GLANTZ: I wasn't challenging you.

ROSSI: Telling me I won't do something because I'm afraid of the consequences isn't a challenge?

GLANTZ: Only if you take it that way.

ROSSI: How would *you* take it?

GLANTZ: I don't think either one of us would ever do or say anything that'd threaten what we have. Okay?

ROSSI: That isn't what you said.

GLANTZ: It's what I meant. *(Reprising what he's typed.)* Seventh victim. Something about the corpse makes Mooney think of first victim's neighbor. *(To Rossi.)* And then?

ROSSI: The Chief, unhappy with Mooney's progress, assigns a Detective Lopez to assist him which pisses Mooney until he meets her.

GLANTZ: Her?

ROSSI: We're half way through the picture and there's no love interest. Lopez is a her.

GLANTZ: I like.

ROSSI: I'm glad.

GLANTZ: Needless to say, Mooney and Lopez hate each other at first sight.

ROSSI: But there's mutual respect because of their outstanding records.

GLANTZ: Plus unmistakable sexual attraction.

ROSSI: Which they fight.

GLANTZ: Because Lopez is newly divorced with a kid.

ROSSI: And Mooney's fiancée just dumped him when he refused to quit the force and accept her father's cushy offer.

GLANTZ: Mooney and Lopez go to grill the junkie who wouldn't say anything before. But now maybe he will because Lopez is Hispanic.

ROSSI: Maybe they grew up together.

GLANTZ: Entering the junkie's apartment they discover the eighth victim.

ROSSI: Another gorgeous woman with the strange teeth marks—her negligee at half mast.

GLANTZ: No.

ROSSI: She's not gorgeous?

GLANTZ: She's gorgeous but?

ROSSI: She's mortally wounded but not dead.

GLANTZ: No.

ROSSI: I give up.

GLANTZ: The gorgeous woman is not a woman.

ROSSI: You're not gonna tell me the junkie is a transvestite.

GLANTZ: Why not?

ROSSI: It's been done to death.

GLANTZ: You got something better?

ROSSI: Not at the moment.

GLANTZ: So I'll put it down for the time being with one addition.

ROSSI: Which is?

GLANTZ: In the eighth victim's lifeless hand, Mooney and Lopez find something we planted early in the story but didn't know how to get back to.

ROSSI: *(Ponders—then makes the connection delightedly.) The diamond that was swiped in the opening scene!*

GLANTZ: Bull's-eye! *(He types furiously.)* Eighth victim…Diamond in hand… Hispanic junkie…Possible transvestite.

ROSSI: Where did the diamond come from?

GLANTZ: The museum.

ROSSI: I mean whose idea was it?

GLANTZ: The diamond? How should I know?

ROSSI: How long we been working on this?

GLANTZ: Six weeks.

ROSSI: If we don't know who came up with a key plot element six weeks ago, how are we supposed to remember who wrote a line thirteen years ago?

GLANTZ: Here we go again.

ROSSI: It really pisses me.

GLANTZ: Obviously.

ROSSI: I know how we can end it. An ad in *Variety* stating we have no idea who's responsible for "Give the bishop my faint regards."

GLANTZ: Better yet a skywriter.

ROSSI: Full page with our signatures.

GLANTZ: You're kidding…You're not kidding.

ROSSI: Well?

GLANTZ: People would think it's a publicity stunt.

ROSSI: I'll pay for the whole thing.

GLANTZ: If I don't participate it's because I'm cheap?

ROSSI: What other reason could there be?

GLANTZ: Maybe I don't want to be a laughing stock.

ROSSI: Maybe you secretly believe the line is yours.

GLANTZ: Do you hear the music from "Twilight Zone"?

ROSSI: The ad would prevent either of us from claiming credit if the other one died first.

GLANTZ: Oh boy.

ROSSI: *(Facing him squarely.)* Do you think "Give the bishop my faint regards" was your idea?

GLANTZ: What did Kipling say about keeping your cool when all about you are losing theirs?

ROSSI: *Yes or no?*

GLANTZ: *(Right arm raised with a sincerity that the gesture, playful in itself, doesn't diminish.)* As God is my judge, I don't think I wrote "Give the bishop my faint regards." Okay?

ROSSI: Okay.

GLANTZ: Shall we proceed.

ROSSI: I've lost the thread.

GLANTZ: *(Reading.)* "Junkie eighth victim. Diamond in hand."

ROSSI: The killer knows the diamond can be traced to him.

GLANTZ: Which might lure him back to the crime scene.

ROSSI: Which Mooney and Lopez, anticipating, have staked out.

GLANTZ: While they're waiting for the killer to return they converse. Find out what each other are really like.

ROSSI: As they share intimate details of their lives they get the hots. Before they know it they're making it.

GLANTZ: With the body still lying there?

ROSSI: Maybe it's a turn-on.

GLANTZ: Boo.

ROSSI: The body's gone and they're about to make it when the phone rings.

GLANTZ: Better. *(He types.)* Mooney and Lopez embracing feverishly... *(He stops typing; looks up.)*

ROSSI: *(Prompting.)* When the phone rings.

GLANTZ: I know.

ROSSI: Put it down.

(Glantz doesn't react.)

ROSSI: What's the matter?

GLANTZ: Did I just swear that I didn't write "Give the bishop my faint regards" or was I dreaming?

ROSSI: It's twenty to four.

GLANTZ: What was that all about?

ROSSI: Nothing.

GLANTZ: You gave me the third degree for nothing?

ROSSI: Don't make a federal case.

GLANTZ: I feel compromised.

ROSSI: I overreacted. Apologies.

GLANTZ: Why did I submit? Why didn't I just say fuck you?

ROSSI: Mooney and Lopez getting it on when the phone rings.

GLANTZ: Fuck you.

ROSSI: Feel better?

GLANTZ: I read somewhere if a person directs your attention to a corner it's because there's something in that corner they want you to see *or* there's something in another corner they *don't* want you to see.

ROSSI: Want to work or you want to bullshit?

GLANTZ: Nice twist if *you* think *you* wrote it and accusing me was projection.

ROSSI: Re-enter Sigmund.

GLANTZ: Meaning?

ROSSI: Spare me the psycho babble.

GLANTZ: Still threatened by my analysis—well, well, well.

ROSSI: Do we let Mooney answer the phone or what?

GLANTZ: We don't do anything until you tell me my imagination is working overtime.

ROSSI: Your imagination is working overtime.

GLANTZ: I'm not convinced.

ROSSI: The clock is ticking.

GLANTZ: Do *you* think *you* wrote "Give the bishop my faint regards?"

ROSSI: Don't be ridiculous.

GLANTZ: Why is it ridiculous when *I* ask but not when you do?

ROSSI: The answer's no.

GLANTZ: Swear like I did you have no idea who wrote it...Well?

ROSSI: I can't.

GLANTZ: Know what's going through my mind?

ROSSI: It's not what you think.

GLANTZ: I'm on a plane. Everything running smooth when the pilot announces one of the engines is on fire.

ROSSI: I swear I don't think I wrote "Give the bishop my faint regards."

GLANTZ: Why didn't you say so before?

ROSSI: That isn't what you asked before.

GLANTZ: I asked you to swear you have no idea who wrote it.

ROSSI: Exactly.

GLANTZ: *(Studying Rossi.)* ...Wait a minute.

ROSSI: A light dawns.

GLANTZ: You didn't write it but you know who did?

ROSSI: By George he's got it.

GLANTZ: *I* wrote it?

ROSSI: No.

GLANTZ: Who then?

(Rossi takes a folded page, green, eight by ten, from his wallet; hands it to Glantz who unfolds it.)

GLANTZ: What's this?

ROSSI: A page from the shooting script. I call your attention to the second speech from the bottom.

GLANTZ: *(Reading.)* "Kindly convey my felicitations to his eminence." *(Turns to Rossi.)* "Kindly convey my felicitations to his eminence"? Ugh. Who wrote that?

ROSSI: We did. Turn it over.

(Glantz turns the page over.)

ROSSI: What do you see?

GLANTZ: A note scribbled in green ink that's practically illegible.

ROSSI: Allow me. *(Taking the page from Glantz he reads.)* "Miles called from the set for a line change he needed immediately. Neither of you reachable, I took it upon myself to come up with something which you may not like but I'm sure it's better than anything Miles would have devised. Signed 'S.' P.S.: Taking a late lunch—back at three."

GLANTZ: "S" as in Sophie?

ROSSI: Yes.

GLANTZ: *(As though struck a body blow.)* You're telling me that the only thing we're going to be remembered for was written by our secretary?

ROSSI: Yes.

GLANTZ: I don't believe it.

ROSSI: Neither did I at first.

GLANTZ: *(Takes the page—reexamines it.)* How long you had this?

ROSSI: Since I moved to the condo—was weeding out my files.

GLANTZ: Six months and you never told me.

ROSSI: I was waiting for the right moment.

GLANTZ: *(Thinks he has it.)* This has gotta be a gag. It's a gag right?

ROSSI: Look in the file. Check the handwriting.

GLANTZ: *(Regarding the note.)* She says she rewrote a line. She doesn't say which line.

ROSSI: You don't see a resemblance between "Give the bishop my faint regards" and "Convey my felicitations to his eminence"?

GLANTZ: Let's assume for the moment you're right.

ROSSI: There's no assume. Sophie wrote it.

GLANTZ: Our Sophie?

ROSSI: Our Sophie.

GLANTZ: Sophie Koslow?

ROSSI: Sophie Koslow.

GLANTZ: Who couldn't type, couldn't spell and screwed up all our phone messages. That Sophie?

ROSSI: That Sophie.

GLANTZ: What happens now?

ROSSI: We have two choices. We either maintain the status quo or go public.

GLANTZ: Which do you recommend?

ROSSI: Status quo.

GLANTZ: Mum's the word.

ROSSI: Right.

GLANTZ: You feel that way why didn't you just get rid of it. Why tell me about it?

ROSSI: It's a decision affecting the both of us.

GLANTZ: Share the guilt in other words.

ROSSI: Isn't that what partners are for?

GLANTZ: What if I decide to announce it to the world—give Sophie her due?

ROSSI: She's been dead for years. What's the point?

GLANTZ: Maybe I want to do something noble before I die.

ROSSI: What script is that from?

GLANTZ: Don't tempt me.

ROSSI: I'll make it easy for you. *(He takes out the card the interviewer gave him thrusts it at Glantz.)* Here's that interviewer's card. You want to do right by Sophie, call her. Give her the scoop.
(Glantz hesitates.)

ROSSI: What's the matter—cat got your balls?
(Glantz grabs the card: goes to the phone; dials.)

ROSSI: I can see it now. "Rossi and Glantz confess secretary wrote 'Give the bishop my faint regards.'" But don't worry, our grandchildren will be thrilled to learn what we *did* write was "Convey my felicitations to his eminence."
(Glantz hangs up.)

ROSSI: Status quo?

GLANTZ: Status quo.

ROSSI: *(Tears the page with Sophie's note in half. Hands the torn pieces to Glantz.)* Your turn.
(Glantz tears the halves into quarters and then into eighths.)

ROSSI: The ashtray.
(Glantz deposits the pieces in an ashtray on the desk. Rossi takes out a cigarette lighter; ignites them. They watch the fire mesmerized.)

GLANTZ: You think God will punish us?

ROSSI: We work for Vogel. It would be excessive.

GLANTZ: We better get busy.

ROSSI: Where were we?

GLANTZ: The crime scene. Mooney and Lopez getting it on when the phone rings.
(A knock at the door interrupts him.)

ROSSI: Come in.
(The woman who interviewed them enters.)

INTERVIEWER: I know how busy you guys are and I apologize.

ROSSI: Let me guess: You have one more question.

INTERVIEWER: No.

GLANTZ: What then?

INTERVIEWER: I lost something and the only place it can be is here. *(She examines the chair she sat in; feels under the cushion without success.)* Damn.

ROSSI: If you tell us what you're looking for maybe we can help.

INTERVIEWER: *(On her hands and knees she reaches under the chair. Her expression goes from anxiety to profound relief.)* Amen! *(Her hand emerges from under the chair bearing the cassette recorder.)* Must have fallen out when I dropped my bag. Thanks again.

(Before Rossi or Glantz can react, she's gone.)

ROSSI: Voice activated?

GLANTZ: And guaranteed to pick up anything within fifty feet.

ROSSI: *(Looking to heaven.)* Touché.

GLANTZ: *(Following Rossi's gaze.)* What he said.

THE END

FORE

INTRODUCTION

Another one from Bungalow 13 at Fox.

Unlike the others, this one actually took place at that site.

I was working for Dick Powell after his remarkable transition from singer to noir private eye and finally director-producer in which capacity I met him.

The older writer, with numerous liberties taken, derives from the late John Fante, a talented novelist and short-story writer (detoured somewhat by Hollywood) who would be delighted by the posthumous renaissance his work now enjoys.

John and I shared that bungalow for several months.

It was he, a fanatic golfer at one time, who initiated the game on the lawn, sprinkler heads as holes.

For me, a neophyte to Hollywood, it was pure lark. Dick Powell regularly asked me what I'd shot.

John and I got on well which made his suddenly moving out a puzzlement until his agent, unaware John had departed, came to me and said, "You're a kid. You want to fool around on the lawn and get fired, that's your business. But John can't afford it."

In that instant I understood and the play was born.

Like the younger writer, I felt compelled, for the good of my soul, to continue playing. I did so for a few days, but absent John the fun was gone and the expressions of passersby (previously unnoticed) began to register as hostile.

Hooray for Hollywood!

ORIGINAL PRODUCTION

Fore was presented at the Ensemble Studio Theatre Marathon in 1993. The play was directed by David Margulies with the following cast:

Drummond	M. Emmett Walsh
Towers	Sam Coppola
Edna	Barbara Andras
Sloan	Ted Neustadt

Time: 1960, mid-morning. Place: A writer's bungalow, some distance from the main buildings, at a major film studio in Hollywood. The bungalow consists of two writers' offices separated by the room their secretaries share. A screen door, upstage, in the center room opens on a lawn.

At rise: the writers' offices (Austin Drummond's at stage left; George Sloan's at stage right) are unoccupied. In the center room, Edna, Drummond's secretary, is typing. The desk reserved for Sloan's secretary is vacant. Through the screen door and windows, we catch glimpses of Drummond, fifty-five, and Sloan, early thirties, bearing putters as they play golf (employing sprinkler indentations as holes) on the lawn.

DRUMMOND: That has to be one of the worst shots I've ever seen.

SLOAN: Thanks.

DRUMMOND: What do you lie?

SLOAN: Three

DRUMMOND: Three?

SLOAN: The shot that hit the tree. The one to the path. And this one.

DRUMMOND: You're still away…Just a minute.

SLOAN: What?

DRUMMOND: You can't touch that ball.

SLOAN: I thought we agreed—

DRUMMOND: —Providing it's less than a foot from the fountain.

SLOAN: Are you saying it's *more* than a foot?

DRUMMOND: *(Calling.)* Edna.

(Edna takes a ruler from the desk; opens the screen doors tosses the ruler to them; returns to the desk; resumes typing.)

DRUMMOND: *(After measurement.)* Voilà! Fire away.

(Sloan poised to shoot.)

DRUMMOND: I've always been an excellent judge of distance.

(Sloan repositions after the interruption about to shoot again.)

DRUMMOND: It runs in the family…Something wrong?

SLOAN: Let me know when you're through.

DRUMMOND: Nerves in one so young. Pity.

SLOAN: *(Strokes—the sound of putter against ball.)* Get up there.

(A beat—then.)

DRUMMOND: Close but no cigar.

SLOAN: I'll give you the hole.

DRUMMOND: Which gives me the game.

(They enter the bungalow.)

EDNA: Well?

DRUMMOND: Score another one for our side.

(Edna takes a notebook from the desk drawer—makes an entry.)

DRUMMOND: If I'm not mistaken that's three in a row.

EDNA: Correct.

SLOAN: *(To Edna.)* Would you mind giving the standings-overall?

EDNA: Eighteen to fifteen.

SLOAN: Leaving me two shy of ultimate victory.

DRUMMOND: *(Exiting into his office.)* Three in a row—six out of the last seven.

SLOAN: *Eighteen to fifteen.*

(The door closes after Drummond—reopens almost immediately.)

DRUMMOND: Lunch—twelve-thirty?

SLOAN: Fine.

DRUMMOND: Give 'em hell.

SLOAN: You too.

(Drummond closes his door. Sloan enters his office—does the same. Sloan drops a golf ball to the floor; taps it with his putter; lays the putter on his desk; picks up a clipboard; flops on a sofa; works in pencil. Drummond goes to his typewriter; regards the contents of a sheet inserted in the carriage; frowns; moves to the center of the room; stands thoughtfully; returns to the typewriter; rechecks the inserted page; moves to a cellotex story board; removes several push pins; backs away; tosses the pins at the board in desultory fashion; has a thought; returns to the desk; sits; pulls the page in progress; crumples it; throws it at a trash basket; inserts a new page; types a few words; regards them; types a bit more; stops; checks; now, increasingly enthused; types without interruption. Charlie Towers, sixty, enters the outer office.)

TOWERS: Good morning.

EDNA: Morning.

TOWERS: *(Indicating Drummond's door.)* Is he in?

(Edna buzzes. Drummond picks up the phone.)

DRUMMOND: Yes?

EDNA: Mr. Towers is here.

DRUMMOND: Towers?…Towers?

EDNA: Your agent.

DRUMMOND: Impossible. My agent vanished months ago. Describe him.

(Towers enters Drummond's office—closes the door.)

DRUMMOND: You've aged.

TOWERS: I stopped in last week—you were gone.

DRUMMOND: I have a phone.

TOWERS: I don't like to disturb you.

DRUMMOND: You're too kind. What's the occasion?

TOWERS: Just wanted to see how you were doing.

DRUMMOND: Fine.

TOWERS: They bought that new book about the Incas for Vogel. Make good on this one and I think I can get it for you.

DRUMMOND: Incas are out of my line.

TOWERS: Then we'll get you something else. The point is Vogel likes you. Pull this one off and you're set. Maybe even a multiple deal.

DRUMMOND: What's up Charlie?

TOWERS: What?

DRUMMOND: Years ago when I still believed that what I had to say warranted a journal, I made a note: "Charlie Towers, when upset, removes his glasses, fingers them nervously."

TOWERS: *(Aware of the glasses in his hand.)* It's a habit—I do it all the time. *(Puts the glasses on.)* Feel better?

DRUMMOND: No bad news?

TOWERS: No bad news.

DRUMMOND: Scout's honor?

TOWERS: I swear.

(Drummond emits a sigh of relief.)

TOWERS: I'm sorry I upset you—I had no idea...

DRUMMOND: That I was so shaky?

(An awkward moment until Drummond laughs.)

TOWERS: How about lunch—we'll go off the lot?

DRUMMOND: I've got a date.

TOWERS: Maybe next week?

DRUMMOND: If you're still inclined.

TOWERS: Why wouldn't I be?

DRUMMOND: Given the fickle nature of the business I'm loath to presume.

TOWERS: Tuesday. Polo Lounge—one p.m. Date?

DRUMMOND: Our first in a year and the Polo Lounge. I'm overwhelmed.

TOWERS: Assuming that means yes, I repeat "Vogel likes you" and depart.

DRUMMOND: He actually said that?

TOWERS: Verbatim. And I can't tell you how glad I am.

DRUMMOND: That makes five of us including ex-wives testy about delinquent payments.

TOWERS: Two of whom could have been avoided.

DRUMMOND: If I'd listened to you?

TOWERS: Among others.

DRUMMOND: Water under the bridge, Charlie. On which note, returning to the muse, adieu.

TOWERS: See you Tuesday.

DRUMMOND: Tuesday it is.

TOWERS: *(Starts to exit; spots the putter; picks it up.)* Yours?

DRUMMOND: Yes.

TOWERS: I had no idea you played.

DRUMMOND: I don't. It's the only club I own. Use it to relax between inspirations. Sank a forty footer this morning.

TOWERS: *(Eyeing the dimensions of the office which are considerably less than forty feet.)* Forty?

DRUMMOND: On the lawn.

TOWERS: The lawn outside?

DRUMMOND: No—the lawn inside.

(Towers shakes his head reproachfully.)

DRUMMOND: What's the matter?

TOWERS: *You* tell *me.*

DRUMMOND: I shouldn't play on the lawn.

TOWERS: Think how it looks.

DRUMMOND: I'm turning out more and better work than I have in years.

TOWERS: What's that got to do with it?

DRUMMOND: I'm not goofing off.

TOWERS: Who said you were? All I'm saying is that it doesn't look right and if I were you I'd stop.

DRUMMOND: You're *not* me.

TOWERS: *(Gesturing toward Sloan's office.)* If that kid Sloan wants—

DRUMMOND: —Sloan?

TOWERS: Isn't that his name?

DRUMMOND: I never mentioned Sloan.

TOWERS: Now look Austin—

DRUMMOND: —Who am I talking to Charlie?

TOWERS: No one sent me if that's what you mean.

DRUMMOND: Nice the way you "discovered" the putter. Could be you missed your calling.

TOWERS: Suppose everyone played golf on the lawn?

DRUMMOND: If it increased the quantity and quality of their work, as it does mine, why not?

TOWERS: You haven't had a credit in four years.

DRUMMOND: I'm talking about *this* job.

TOWERS: You know what people will think?

DRUMMOND: What people?

TOWERS: He's back on the sauce.

DRUMMOND: I haven't had a drop in fourteen weeks.

TOWERS: Up to his old tricks.

DRUMMOND: Ask Vogel what he thinks of the pages I turned in last week.

TOWERS: It's got nothing to do with the pages.

DRUMMOND: Phoned me at home to say how much he liked them.

TOWERS: Austin!

(He gains Drummonds's attention.)

TOWERS: Give it up.

DRUMMOND: If and when Vogel asks me to, I'll think about it. Until then—

TOWERS: —Consider yourself asked.

(Drummond regards him incredulously.)

TOWERS: Yes—

DRUMMOND: *(Mimicking bitterly.)* "Nobody sent me if that's what you mean."

TOWERS: He likes you, likes your work, couldn't care less how you spend your time—

DRUMMOND: —But.

TOWERS: His own position isn't too secure. Suppose the old man saw you?

DRUMMOND: Why did he go through you?

TOWERS: He didn't want to make an issue.

DRUMMOND: Is it an issue?

TOWERS: That's up to you.

DRUMMOND: Instead of a coffee break or sneaking out for a drink we tap a golf ball around. What could be more innocent?

TOWERS: You had no idea you were off base?

DRUMMOND: Not at first.

TOWERS: Then you did know.

DRUMMOND: People began to watch us. They smiled, but I thought I detected a faint odor of resentment.

TOWERS: Why didn't you stop?

DRUMMOND: I was enjoying myself—besides I might have been mistaken.

TOWERS: What about Sloan?

DRUMMOND: It's his first studio job. Fresh from New York he thinks he died and went to heaven. Hasn't the foggiest we're doing anything wrong.

TOWERS: You didn't tell him?

DRUMMOND: I hate people who try to diminish their fears by spreading them.

TOWERS: You might be doing him a favor.

DRUMMOND: He's read every book and story I ever published!

TOWERS: What's that got to do with it?

DRUMMOND: Nothing.

TOWERS: …What are you going to do?

DRUMMOND: I haven't decided.

TOWERS: I wasn't supposed to bring Vogel's name into it.

DRUMMOND: Don't worry.

TOWERS: I hope you're not going to do anything foolish.

DRUMMOND: So do I.

TOWERS: You were out of work seven months before this job.

DRUMMOND: Nine.

TOWERS: He really likes you.

DRUMMOND: And he's got a book about Incas recalling the Jewish writer unable to do a cowboy and Indian picture until the producer told him to think of the latter as Nazis.

TOWERS: Stop playing on the lawn or you're out.

DRUMMOND: That's plain enough.

TOWERS: I hope so.

DRUMMOND: How do I break the news to Sloan without losing what little remains of my face?

TOWERS: You'll think of something.

DRUMMOND: If I told you I resent your certainty, would we still be on for Tuesday?

TOWERS: If you're still working here. If not I have a previous engagement.

DRUMMOND: Candid to a flaw.

TOWERS: That's me. Gotta run. *(He starts to leave.)*

DRUMMOND: Charlie…

(Towers turns to him.)

DRUMMOND: Isn't there a secret part of you that hopes I go on playing?

TOWERS: We all didn't go to Princeton.

DRUMMOND: I keep forgetting.

(Towers exits; closes the door; departs the bungalow. Drummond stands as he is for some time; then moves to his desk; picks up a script; thumbs to a particular page; removes that page and the two which follow from the folder; enters the outer office.)

DRUMMOND: *(To Edna.)* Would you mind taking your lunch hour now?

EDNA: It's not even twelve.

DRUMMOND: I'll need you before one.

(She rises reluctantly.)

DRUMMOND: Thank you.

(She exits. Drummond goes to Sloan's door; hesitates; knocks.)

SLOAN: Come in.

DRUMMOND: (Enters.) Got a minute?

SLOAN: Sure…What's up?

DRUMMOND: A favor.

SLOAN: Shoot.

DRUMMOND: (Extending the three pages.) Read this scene. See if it's clear.

(Sloan makes no move to take the pages.)

DRUMMOND: What's the matter?

SLOAN: I'd rather not.

DRUMMOND: Three pages—take you a minute.

SLOAN: It's not that.

DRUMMOND: What then?

SLOAN: I don't think it's a good idea.

DRUMMOND: Why not?

SLOAN: I don't like anyone to see my work till it's finished.

DRUMMOND: This is *my* work.

SLOAN: I don't think it's a good idea in general.

DRUMMOND: It's simple exposition. I just want to be sure it's clear.

SLOAN: I'm sorry but I—

DRUMMOND: — Afraid it might give you an inferiority complex?

SLOAN: That's it.

DRUMMOND: Are you sure?

SLOAN: What do you mean?

DRUMMOND: Maybe it's just the opposite: You're afraid the old master's lost his touch.

SLOAN: Austin, we get along fine—why make waves?

DRUMMOND: Not much of a relationship if it can't survive the reading of three pages.

SLOAN: …You just want to know if it's clear?

DRUMMOND: That's all.

(Sloan reaches out.)

DRUMMOND: (Handing him the pages.) Thanks.

(While Sloan reads, Drummond takes his putter and practices. Sloan finishes reading.)

DRUMMOND: Well?

SLOAN: Yes.

DRUMMOND: Yes?

SLOAN: It's clear.

DRUMMOND: What's clear?

SLOAN: Someone named Casey overhears a conversation in which the murder of a man named Alvarez is discussed. You learn that Alvarez was a wealthy man whose source of wealth was a mystery.

DRUMMOND: Go on.

SLOAN: That's it.

DRUMMOND: I see.

SLOAN: Did I miss something?

DRUMMOND: *(Reclaiming the pages.)* No.

SLOAN: I *did* miss something.

DRUMMOND: No.

SLOAN: Let me read it again.

DRUMMOND: *You didn't miss anything.*

SLOAN: Then what's the matter?

DRUMMOND: *(Sarcastic.)* I thought you might have something to say about the spelling and punctuation.

SLOAN: You said you were only interested in clarity.

DRUMMOND: That was to get you to read it…Well?

SLOAN: You want my opinion of the scene.

DRUMMOND: Yes.

SLOAN: It seems fine.

DRUMMOND: Seems?

SLOAN: Is.

DRUMMOND: *Don't slough me.*

SLOAN: Three pages from the middle of a script I haven't read —what do you expect me to say?

DRUMMOND: Would you like to read the rest of the script?

SLOAN: No.

DRUMMOND: The scene didn't hook you.

SLOAN: I don't read works in progress—I told you.

DRUMMOND: And you're not the sort to break a rule.

SLOAN: What's that supposed to mean?

DRUMMOND: I spent a week on these pages.

SLOAN: Exposition scenes can be tough.

DRUMMOND: Is that a fact?

SLOAN: Austin—

DRUMMOND: —Why don't you tell me about exposition scenes—I'm sure I'd find it instructive.

SLOAN: *Austin.*

(*Drummond regards him.*)

SLOAN: What is it? What do you want from me?

DRUMMOND: A little respect.

SLOAN: Respect?

DRUMMOND: By the time I was your age I'd written four novels—every one the genuine article.

SLOAN: Four and a half.

(*Drummond looks at him questioningly.*)

SLOAN: I'm thirty-two. By the time you were thirty-two you were working on "The Cruel Time."

DRUMMOND: How do you know that?

SLOAN: I dug up that New Yorker profile you mentioned the other day.

DRUMMOND: To see how the mighty have fallen?

SLOAN: To learn all I can about a man whose work means a lot to me.

DRUMMOND: Now let us bow our heads.

SLOAN: What?

DRUMMOND: Your praise has a funereal air.

SLOAN: Is this a gag?

DRUMMOND: A few stories, a play that will never be produced, and he rules the world.

SLOAN: You said you liked the play.

DRUMMOND: Erring on the side of generosity has long been a failing.

SLOAN: I think you better get out of here.

DRUMMOND: My very thought. (*He starts out—pauses.*) The other day you wondered why I didn't write novels or stories any more. I said the atmosphere wasn't conducive. "Why don't you leave?" you inquired boyishly. To which I mumbled something about intending to do so as soon as I had a nest egg. Well kid I hate to disillusion further but I lied. The fact, as you will discover when you've tarried sufficiently, is that nobody leaves unless they send you away.

SLOAN: *Get out!*

(*Drummond enters the outer office—leaves Sloan's door open; picks up Edna's phone; dials.*)

DRUMMOND: (*On the phone—emphasizing his words for Sloan's benefit.*) This is Austin Drummond...I'm unhappy with my office—too many distractions...Do you have anything available in the main building?... Excellent. I'll have my secretary make the transfer after lunch. (*He hangs up; exits.*)

(Sloan, hurt, confused, slams his door shut; fights to control his feelings. Charlie Towers enters the outer office somewhat furtively; knocks at Sloan's door.)

SLOAN: *(Hopeful that it is Drummond.)* Come in.

TOWERS: *(Enters. Fingering his glasses.)* I'm Charlie Towers—Drummond's agent.

SLOAN: I know.

TOWERS: I wonder if I might have a word with you—in confidence.

SLOAN: About what?

TOWERS: You and him playing golf on the lawn.

SLOAN: What about it?

TOWERS: It doesn't look right. You should stop.

SLOAN: Go on.

TOWERS: *You're* just starting out. If you want to get a bad reputation that's your business—but Drummond can't afford it.

SLOAN: Shouldn't you be saying this to *him?*

TOWERS: I have.

SLOAN: And?

TOWERS: He said he'd think about it.

SLOAN: I see.

TOWERS: I was hoping I could get you to stop the game for his sake.

SLOAN: It's already stopped. He's moving out—taking an office in the main building.

TOWERS: How come?

SLOAN: We had an argument.

TOWERS: What about?

SLOAN: A personal matter.

TOWERS: I'm sorry to hear it—but it's probably for the best.

SLOAN: Probably.

TOWERS: You won't mention it—that I was here.

SLOAN: No.

TOWERS: Hope I didn't bother you.

(Sloan offers no response.)

TOWERS: So long.

(No response from Sloan. Towers exits from the room and the cottage. Sloan stands as he is for a moment; picks up the putter; regards it; now picks up the ball; disappears outdoors. A moment of silence and then we hear.)

SLOAN'S VOICE: Fore!

THE END

GETTING IN

INTRODUCTION

For years I delighted telling the miraculous tale of how I got into Dartmouth. When family and friends got tired of hearing it, I committed it to paper.

The *Dartmouth Alumni Magazine* published it and EST included it in its annual one-act Marathon.

The Duffy in *Getting In* is the nineteen-year-old who surfaces some fifty years later as the Duffy in *Contact with the Enemy* (see Volume One, the full-length collection) recently premiered at EST.

God bless the GI Bill of Rights and Davis and Elkins, the only college of the thirty I applied to that accepted me and where I would have gone if Dartmouth, on what basis I can't fathom, hadn't come through at the eleventh hour.

ORIGINAL PRODUCTION

Getting In was presented at the Ensemble Studio Theatre Marathon in 1997. The play was directed by Chris Smith, sets were by Michael Allen, costumes by Bruce Goodrich, and lighting by Alistair Wandesforde-Smith, with the following cast:

Bill Duffy. . . . . Thomas McHugh

Torelli . . . . Marc Romeo

Whitley . . . . Paul Whitthorne

Dean Strong and Mr. Carswell . . . . Dan Dailey

Secretary and Mrs. Duffy . . . . Polly Adams

Professor Jensen and Dean Chamberlin . . . . Bill Cwikowski

Emily and The WAAC . . . . Melinda Page

Time: April 1945. Place: Somewhere in Germany. At rise: Bill Duffy, nineteen, alert, boyish, an Army PFC, spotlighted on an otherwise dark stage. His accent marks him a New Yorker. Sharper ears might pinpoint the Bronx.

DUFFY: *The war in Europe nearly over, I decided I'd be the first one in my family to go to college. On guard duty, at night, in a forward outpost in Germany, I broke the news to my buddy, Al Torelli.*
(*Lights down on Duffy and up on Al Torelli and Duffy on guard duty. Both with helmets and rifles. Torelli the same age as Duffy but he seems older, Torelli's New York accent more pronounced than Duffy's.*)

TORELLI: …What was that?

DUFFY: What was what?

TORELLI: You didn't hear something?

DUFFY: Like what?

TORELLI: *Keep your voice down.*

DUFFY: What's eating you?

TORELLI: The war's gonna end any day. I don't wanna be the last casualty.

DUFFY: …You see in *Stars and Stripes* about the GI Bill, lets veterans go to college free?

TORELLI: So what?

DUFFY: I'm gonna do it. Go to college.

TORELLI: You barely got through high school.

DUFFY: I'm different now.

TORELLI: What time is it?

DUFFY: Five minutes later than the last time you asked…What about you?

TORELLI: What about me?

DUFFY: What are you gonna do after the war?

TORELLI: Ask me that again I'll bust your jaw!

DUFFY: What did I say?

TORELLI: A pitcher has a no-hitter going, nobody mentions it till the final out so they don't jinx him. That's how I feel talking about my future till the war's officially over. Okay?

DUFFY: Okay.

TORELLI: …How's it work—the GI Bill?

DUFFY: Free tuition, books, room. Plus seventy-five bucks a month!

TORELLI: What college you going to?

DUFFY: I thought the future was off limits.

TORELLI: Mine. Yours I don't give a damn.

DUFFY: If I could go any place I wanted it'd be Dartmouth.

TORELLI: That's one of those Ivy League places like Yale and Harvard.

DUFFY: Right.

TORELLI: Dream on.

DUFFY: *(Defensively.)* I wasn't trying in high school. I—

TORELLI: *—Shut up.*

DUFFY: Now what?

TORELLI: Footsteps. Got your safety on?

DUFFY: Yeah.

TORELLI: Take it off.

DUFFY: I don't hear anything.

TORELLI: *Take it off, God damn it!*

(The click as Duffy prepares his rifle to fire. Silence while both listen. No sound. Then Torelli chuckles.)

DUFFY: What's funny?

TORELLI: You in the Ivy League.

(Lights down on Torelli so only Duffy is seen.)

DUFFY: *The war in Europe ended a week later. I figured I'd be out of the army by the spring of '46 in time to begin college that fall. But I had no idea how to go about applying. Then I heard about this Captain in Division Headquarters who went to Dartmouth.*

(Lights down on Duffy and up on Captain Whitley's office. Whitley, twenty-two, well groomed, patrician features, reading a book and listening to classical music on the radio. A knock at the door.)

WHITLEY: Enter.

(The door opens. Duffy appears.)

DUFFY: *(Saluting crisply.)* Captain Whitley sir?

WHITLEY: *(Returning the salute.)* Yes?

DUFFY: *(At attention.)* PFC Duffy—89th cavalry reconnaissance troop.

WHITLEY: At ease. State your business.

DUFFY: It's a personal matter sir.

WHITLEY: *(Turns the radio off.)* Go on.

DUFFY: I've decided to go to college. Was hoping you might tell me how to go about it.

WHITLEY: Write to the Dean of Admission.

DUFFY: *(Taking notes.)* "Dean of Admissions."

WHITLEY: He'll give you the information you need.

DUFFY: What's his name?

WHITLEY: *(Amused by his apparent ignorance.)* Every college has a different one.

DUFFY: What's the name of the Dean of Admissions at Dartmouth?

WHITLEY: *(Startled.)* Dartmouth?

DUFFY: Yes sir.

WHITLEY: It so happens I'm a Dartmouth man.

DUFFY: That's why I'm here. I figured a Dartmouth graduate could give me some tips.

WHITLEY: I have a year to go before I graduate. Why Dartmouth?

DUFFY: It sounds crazy but I saw this movie—

WHITLEY: ... *Winter Carnival.*

DUFFY: Right. It was love at first sight.

WHITLEY: There's more to Dartmouth than Winter Carnival.

DUFFY: Yes sir. *(Notebook and pen poised.)* The Dean of Admissions name?

WHITLEY: *(Reluctantly.)* Strong.

DUFFY: S-t-r-o-n-g?

WHITLEY: Yes.

DUFFY: First name?

WHITLEY: I don't remember. Where did you go to high school?

DUFFY: New York City.

WHITLEY: *(Alluding to his accent.)* Obviously. I meant *what* school.

DUFFY: DeWitt Clinton.

WHITLEY: Where did you rank?

DUFFY: I don't know.

WHITLEY: You don't know your standing?

DUFFY: There were ten thousand guys at Clinton.

WHITLEY: How were your grades?

DUFFY: I never failed anything.

WHITLEY: Overall average?...Well?

DUFFY: *(Bristling.)* Sixty-six. Sixty-five was passing. Plus if you add up my absences I missed a term because I played hookey. Anything else *sir?*

WHITLEY: I'm trying to help you soldier.

DUFFY: It's three years since high school. I've changed.

WHITLEY: *(Insinuating.)* It's the GI Bill, isn't it?

DUFFY: *(Pointedly.)* Right. I'm going to college because it's a free ride. Plus I noticed college guys get the best jobs in the Army where they have the least chance of getting killed.

WHITLEY: *You're dismissed soldier.*

DUFFY: *(Saluting.)* Thank you *sir. (He starts to exit—looks back.)* Are you going back to Dartmouth to get your degree?

WHITLEY: Yes.

DUFFY: Maybe I'll see you there.

(Before Whitley can react, he's gone. Lights down on Whitley looking after him. Lights up on Duffy reading a letter aloud.)

DUFFY: *"Dean of Admissions, Dartmouth College, Hanover, New Hampshire—October 13, 1945. Dear Dean Strong, I am writing you from Austria where I'm on occupation duty after serving in General Patton's Third Army during the war. I expect to be discharged next spring and would like to apply for admission to Dartmouth in the fall of 1946. Could you please advise me how to proceed. Sincerely PFC William Duffy."*

(Lights up on Dean Strong, mid-fifties, avuncular, caring.)

DEAN STRONG: *"Dear Private Duffy. Enclosed is an application for admission. I am pleased by your interest in Dartmouth but feel it only fair to inform you that we expect no less than five thousand applications for some six hundred places. Best wishes. Dean Robert Strong."*

DUFFY: *"Dear Dean Strong, My application is enclosed. As you can see my high school grades leave much to be desired. The idea of going to college never crossed my mind in high school. In the years since I've undergone a complete turnaround."*

DEAN STRONG: *"Dear William Duffy, I sense your about face is genuine and applaud you for it, but I would be derelict if I didn't emphasize that your chances of gaining admission are minimal. I strongly urge you not to focus all your hopes on Dartmouth and enclose a catalog of accredited colleges and universities you should consider."*

DUFFY: *"Dear Dean Strong, I appreciate your warning about the slimness of my chances and will apply to other places. But Dartmouth will always be my first choice."*

DEAN STRONG: *"Dear William, I'm touched by your determination and sorry I can't offer you more hope."*

DUFFY: *"Dear Dean Strong, In a few days I'll be homeward bound. Would it be possible to visit Dartmouth? I'd like to see it and thank you for your considerate attention."*

DEAN STRONG: *"Dear William, Interviews can be helpful but high school records carry the most weight. I put this bluntly so you don't contemplate the trip with false hopes or expectations."*

(Lights down on Dean Strong. Lights up on Duffy in the changing room of a clothing store. Only his head and shoulders visible above the partial door as he switches from army uniform to civilian clothes. As he speaks, he dons shirt and tie—the rest of the change hidden from view.)

DUFFY: On the troop ship coming home, I won thirty-four hundred bucks in a crap game. I asked my father to try and find someone with Dartmouth con-

nections. He said he met a guy in a bar whose nephews were Dartmouth graduates and they'd give my name to a Professor I should look up when I visited Dartmouth. I debated whether I should let Dean Strong know I was coming. I decided to surprise him…Wanting to make a good impression, I spent some of my crap game winnings on a new suit. Not just new but tailor-made by the guy who did Whitey Bloom's clothes—Whitey, a bookie, the best dresser in the neighborhood. (Donning the jacket, Duffy proudly emerges from the changing room in a blue pinstripe suit befitting a bookmaker but definitely not Ivy League.) Boarding the train at Grand Central I had a sense of new beginnings. The trip like a dream until we reached White River Junction. How could such an ugly railhead be only a few miles from Dartmouth, which looked like heaven in every picture I'd ever seen? I got in a cab and minutes later there it was: the campus. The white buildings. The library where bells tolled the hour. Everything as advertised. I checked into The Green Lantern and headed for the Admissions Building.
(Lights down on Duffy and up on an office where a Secretary is typing. A knock at the door interrupts her.)

SECRETARY: Come in.

(Duffy enters.)

DUFFY: Dean Strong's office?

SECRETARY: Yes.

DUFFY: My name's William Duffy. I've been corresponding with the Dean about getting into Dartmouth. He invited me to visit him when I got out of the army. Here I am.

(The Secretary just looks at him.)

DUFFY: I should have written I was coming but I made up my mind all of a sudden. Is there any chance I could see him?

(The Secretary offers no reaction.)

DUFFY: It doesn't have to be right now. I'm staying overnight. And if he's busy tomorrow, I'll stay longer.

SECRETARY: (Tears welling.) Oh dear.

DUFFY: What's the matter?

SECRETARY: Dean Strong is dead.

DUFFY: Dean Strong?

SECRETARY: Yes.

DUFFY: (Incredulous.) When—how?

SECRETARY: Last week. A heart attack.

(Lights down on the Secretary.)

DUFFY: I left the office in a daze, figuring, "That's the end of me and Dartmouth."

Then I remembered the guy whose nephews went to Dartmouth and the professor they said I should look up.

(Lights up on Professor Jensen, fifty, as he answers a ringing phone.)

PROFESSOR JENSEN: Hello?

DUFFY: *(In a pay phone.)* Professor Jensen?

PROFESSOR JENSEN: Speaking.

DUFFY: My name is Duffy—William Duffy. *(Regarding a card.)* I'm a friend of the Dexter brothers—Harry and Raymond.

PROFESSOR JENSEN: *(Remembering.)* Duffy—right.

DUFFY: I'm trying to get into Dartmouth. They said you might be able to help me.

PROFESSOR JENSEN: As I told the Dexters, there's very little if anything I can do. What I suggest is you send me your records and…

DUFFY: …I'm here.

PROFESSOR JENSEN: Here?

DUFFY: In Hanover. I was hoping I might meet you.

PROFESSOR JENSEN: You picked a busy week.

DUFFY: I could make it any time—right now if it's convenient.

PROFESSOR JENSEN: I'm on my way out.

DUFFY: I understand. *(Eyeing the card.)* I'll tell Harry and Ray I got you at a bad time. Sorry I bothered you.

PROFESSOR JENSEN: *(Feeling he's been too abrupt.)* How are they?

DUFFY: Harry and Ray? They're fine.

PROFESSOR JENSEN: Still avid tennis players?

DUFFY: Yes.

PROFESSOR JENSEN: I never won a set from either of them.

DUFFY: *(Figuring he has nothing to lose.)* They said you were pretty good.

PROFESSOR JENSEN: *(Delighted.)* They did?

DUFFY: Yes. They spoke about Dartmouth a lot. That's what made me apply. Well, listen, it's been nice talking to you. I'll give them your regards.

PROFESSOR JENSEN: Who you should speak to is the Dean of Admissions.

DUFFY: That's what I came for but he's dead.

PROFESSOR JENSEN: I mean the Acting Dean. He's swamped but he happens to be a friend of mine. Where are you staying?

DUFFY: The Green Lantern.

PROFESSOR JENSEN: I'll try and get you an appointment. But don't count on it.

(Lights down on Professor Jensen.)

DUFFY: *Figuring he was just going through the motions and I'd never see this place again, I walked around memorizing everything: The campus where fraternity teams were playing softball; the tree-lined streets with dormitories where there were white shoes on window sills—guys hollering and laughing. Then I came to the stadium and sat in the stands imagining what it would be like during a football game with the band and cheering. Finally an old red building where the Glee Club was rehearsing a song that was so moving I cried because I knew this was the place I wanted to be more than anywhere in the world and there was no chance of it happening. (Blows his nose to regain composure.) After supper I decided to buy some magazines and call it a day. (Lights down on Duffy and up in a drugstore where Emily, nineteen, wholesomely attractive in nurse's uniform, is perusing a rack of paperback books as Duffy appears beside her.)*

DUFFY: *(As she takes a book from the rack.)* I hope you're buying that book for someone else.

EMILY: Why?

DUFFY: It's science fiction.

EMILY: So what?

DUFFY: I could never love a woman who likes science fiction.

EMILY: *(Jocularly.)* As a matter of fact I'm buying it for a patient.

DUFFY: Amen. I'm about to have a soda and I hate to drink alone. Join me?

EMILY: Thanks but I go on duty at the hospital in twenty minutes.

DUFFY: If I had a car I'd offer you a ride.

EMILY: It's a ten minute walk.

DUFFY: Mind if I join you.

EMILY: Suit yourself.

(Lights down on Emily.)

DUFFY: *As we walked I told her I was trying to get into Dartmouth. She wished me luck—gave me her name and phone number. I said I'd call her if I succeeded. (Reads the card she gave him.) "Emily Wilkens." I was about to put it in my wallet when I got this notion that if I tore up the card it would help me—like a sacrificial offering. (He tears up the card.) When I got back to the Green Lantern there was a message.*

(Lights down on Duffy and up on Professor Jensen.)

PROFESSOR JENSEN: You have a nine A.M. meeting with Acting Dean of Admissions Chamberlin. He's squeezing you in so be on time. Good luck and my best to Harry and Ray.

(Lights down on the Professor and up on Acting Dean Chamberlin, fortyish, going over documents at his desk when the Secretary appears.)

DEAN CHAMBERLIN: *(Rising, hand extended.)* Good morning.

DUFFY: Good morning sir.

DEAN CHAMBERLIN: *(Indicating a chair in front of the desk.)* Have a seat.
  (Duffy sits. Chamberlin resumes his place behind the desk.)

DEAN CHAMBERLIN: I reviewed your correspondence with Dean Strong, your application, and your high school records. Couldn't find your College Board Scores.

DUFFY: College Board Scores?

DEAN CHAMBERLIN: Yes. Didn't you take the test?

DUFFY: No.

DEAN CHAMBERLIN: You know what the Boards are.

DUFFY: Not exactly.

DEAN CHAMBERLIN: Standard nationwide exams for college entrance. You should have taken them in high school.

DUFFY: I wasn't thinking about college in those days.

DEAN CHAMBERLIN: To get into almost any college but Dartmouth, College Boards are mandatory.

DUFFY: You don't need them for Dartmouth?

DEAN CHAMBERLIN: Not if you're a veteran. Dean Strong didn't think it was fair to make ex-servicemen compete with high school kids to whom the test material is fresh. Instead of College Boards, Dartmouth requires veterans take a general aptitude exam which measures basic intelligence rather than specific subject matter.

DUFFY: Where do I take it?

DEAN CHAMBERLIN: Any Veterans Administration office. *(Indicating Duffy's file.)* It's important but it won't outweigh what's in here. *(Leafing through the file.)* You were absent a great deal...No sports...No extra curricular activities, period...Barely passing grades. *(Holding up a sheaf of envelopes.)* These are the applications that came in since Monday. Everyone in the top ten percent of their class. Several valedictorians. Many with distinguished athletic records. All with superior Board scores.

DUFFY: Making my chances slim to none.

DEAN CHAMBERLIN: I'm afraid so. In one of his letters Dean Strong suggested you not pin all your hopes on Dartmouth. I second that.

DUFFY: I'm going to apply elsewhere but Dartmouth is still my first choice.

DEAN CHAMBERLIN: That's it then. *(Rising—hand outstretched.)* Sorry I can't be more encouraging.

DUFFY: *(Ignoring his hand.)* That's not me.

DEAN CHAMBERLIN: What?

DUFFY: That folder with my high school records. That's who I was. It's not the way I am now.

DEAN CHAMBERLIN: Unfortunately it's all we have to go by.

DUFFY: Would you like to know how and why I changed?

DEAN CHAMBERLIN: Unfortunately I'm pressed for time.

DUFFY: Two minutes?

DEAN CHAMBERLIN: *(Reluctantly.)* Two minutes. *(Resumes his seat.)*

DUFFY: Between high school and the army I was a messenger for a freight forwarder in lower Manhattan. Five and a half days a week running nonstop for twenty-five bucks minus deductions. It took over an hour each way on a packed subway just to get there. One morning on the way to work I feel a sneeze coming on. I want to cover my mouth but I'm jammed in so tight I can't move my hand. I end up sneezing right in this lady's face. That's when it hit me there has to be a better way of life and…

(The Dean's intercom buzzer interrupts.)

DEAN CHAMBERLIN: Pardon me. *(On the intercom.)* Yes?

SECRETARY'S VOICE: Mr. Stewart is here.

DEAN CHAMBERLIN: I'll be right with him. *(To Duffy.)* Why don't you write the rest—send it to me?

DUFFY: You said two minutes.

DEAN CHAMBERLIN: …Go on.

DUFFY: The messenger job made getting drafted a pleasure. I ended up in Patton's Third Army—the last two campaigns before VE Day. Not a lot of action, but enough so I realized I had as much guts as most guys. After the war we stayed in Europe on occupation duty. I'd heard about the GI Bill and wanted to go to college but wondered if I was smart enough. So I enrolled in one of the schools the army set up to keep us busy. Began to read. Not because I had to, but because I enjoyed it. There were tests and I did great. I…

DEAN CHAMBERLIN: *(Indicating his watch.)* …I'm afraid I have to stop you. *(Offering his hand with finality.)* Goodbye and good luck.

DUFFY: *(Taking his hand.)* Thanks for your time. *(He starts to leave then turns to the Dean passionately.)* I know I can do the work if I get in. If I can't I'll leave voluntarily. You want—I'll put it in writing. I need a break! *(He exits.)*

(Lights down on the Dean—his expression suggests Duffy is unique in his experience.)

DUFFY: *Convinced the trip was a fiasco, I told the cab driver to circle the campus for a last look before he took me to White River Junction where I boarded the train and, feeling as low as I can remember, headed for the club car.*

(Lights up on the club car as Duffy sits at one of two side-by-side tables—the other table vacant.)

DUFFY: *It didn't cheer me up when a prosperous looking old guy across the aisle struck up a conversation with a kid wearing a Dartmouth jacket. The old guy tells the young guy he's a Dartmouth graduate. The young guy says he's about to graduate. Turns out the old guy is president of an advertising agency. Within ten minutes the old guy is offering the kid a job. All because they both went to Dartmouth, which they talked about till I couldn't take it any more and was about to leave when...*

(An attractive woman, early twenties in a WAAC uniform with First Lieutenant bars, enters the club car.)

THE WAAC: *(To Duffy—indicating the table beside him.)* Anyone sitting here?

DUFFY: No.

(She sits.)

DUFFY: It's a good thing we didn't meet two weeks ago.

THE WAAC: Why?

DUFFY: I was still in the army—a private. I couldn't have invited you to have a drink.

THE WAAC: Is that what you're doing?

DUFFY: Yes.

THE WAAC: Vodka neat.

DUFFY: *(Calling off.)* Waiter.

(Lights down on the WAAC.)

DUFFY: *She and I drank steadily. The club car was air conditioned and the temperature in New York was over ninety. Getting off the train at Grand Central was like walking into a blast furnace. The booze took its toll and we staggered off in opposite directions. No cab driver would take me because I was reeling so I took the subway. Getting off every few stops to throw up. When I got home, my father said, "You must have made a grand impression at Dartmouth." At which point, mercifully, I passed out...*

(Lights down on Duffy and up on a portable typewriter sitting on a table. Duffy enters.)

DUFFY: *(Touching the typewriter affectionately.)* Royal portable. List price one hundred and twenty-five bucks. I paid one-fifty because they were tough to get and I needed it for college applications because my penmanship was awful. I applied for admission to thirty colleges. Within two weeks, half of them notified me they had no openings. The day before I was scheduled to take the aptitude test at the Veterans' Administration I attended Al Torelli's wedding in Brooklyn.

(Lights down on Duffy and up on Torelli in a tuxedo.)

TORELLI: Surprise you I'm getting married so soon?

DUFFY: Yeah.

TORELLI: *(Accusing.)* You think it's a mistake, and you're right.

DUFFY: You feel like that why go through with it?

TORELLI: I been going with her since high school. You make promises. Besides, her brothers would kill me.

DUFFY: Run away.

TORELLI: Just like that.

DUFFY: I've got fifteen hundred in my wallet. It's yours. There's the door.

TORELLI: My old man's dying. I've got my mother and kid sister to support. But thanks anyway. It's not like I don't love her. Probably nothing but bridegroom jitters. Huh?

DUFFY: Probably.

TORELLI: Something tells me this is the last time you and I will ever see each other.

DUFFY: Why?

TORELLI: In college you'll make new friends—get different ideas.

DUFFY: There's a laugh.

TORELLI: What do you mean?

DUFFY: I've been turned down by fifteen colleges already.

TORELLI: *(With conviction.)* Don't matter. One way or another you're gonna make it.

(Organ music heard.)

TORELLI: There's my cue.

DUFFY: I love you Al.

TORELLI: I love you too. Too bad I'm spoken for.

(Lights down on Torelli.)

DUFFY: *When the priest said the part about anyone knowing why these people shouldn't marry, I felt like jumping up and saying after what he'd been through in the war, Al had the right to live a little before he put his shoulder to the wheel. I left the reception early because the more I drank the more depressed I got about my own future as well as Al's. The next morning at the Veterans' Administration I was directed to the office of a Mr. Carswell.*
(Lights down on Duffy and up on a small conference room where Mr. Carswell, fortyish, officious, impatient, regards his pocket watch irritatedly. A knock at the door.)

CARSWELL: Come in.

(Duffy enters.)

DUFFY: Mr. Carswell?

CARSWELL: You're late.

DUFFY: I was told to be here at nine. *(Glancing at his wristwatch.)* It's five of.

CARSWELL: *(Displaying his pocket watch as final authority.)* It's one minute past. *(Goes into his practiced spiel.)* The exam is in two parts. Multiple choice and essay. Two hours each. The multiple choice section you'll find on the table. At eleven o'clock I'll collect it and give you the essay portion. At no time are you to leave this room without my permission. You may begin. *(Carswell retires to his office.)*

DUFFY: *He left the door of his office open so he could keep track of me. (Duffy sits—opens the question book.) As advertised the questions were aimed at general intelligence rather than subjects you study in high school. I felt I was doing pretty good but still had over fifty questions to go when Mr. Carswell reappeared.*

CARSWELL: *(Regarding his pocket watch.)* In ten seconds it will be eleven o'clock. *(Counting.)* Five-four-three-two-one. I'll take that.

DUFFY: *(Handing him the test.)* Did anybody ever answer all the questions in two hours?

CARSWELL: Yes.

DUFFY: It's rare though, huh?

CARSWELL: Not particularly. *(Hands him several pamphlets.)* Here is the essay part of the exam. Again you have two hours ending at one p.m. You may begin. *(Carswell exits to his office.)*

DUFFY: *What he said about people who answered all the multiple choice questions meant I really had to shine in the essay part. The assigned topic was "Why I Want to go to College". Having thought of nothing else for months, I dove in and got so caught up I forgot about everything including the time which made it a shock when Mr. Carswell appeared.*

CARSWELL: I'll take that now.

DUFFY: *(Regards his watch.)* It's only twelve-thirty.

CARSWELL: Sometimes less is more.

DUFFY: *(Firmly.)* I'm not through.

(Mr. Carswell frowns and withdraws.)

DUFFY: *It took a moment to collect myself during which I heard him on the phone talking to someone named Gladys who must have been giving him a hard time because he's saying things like, "I can't help it," and "I'll do my best, Gladys," in a whiny voice. Then he slammed down the receiver.*

(Mr. Carswell reappears.)

CARSWELL: I have to go upstairs. I'll be back by one o'clock. But if by some chance I'm not, put your essay on my desk.

DUFFY: Right.

CARSWELL: Shouldn't take me more than a few minutes. *(Carswell exits.)*

DUFFY: *I resumed writing. And the next thing I know it's a minute to one. I had a lot more to say but I knew if he found me working after the deadline he'd axe me. So I stopped and was about to put it on his desk when it hit me that Mr. Carswell wasn't coming back for quite a while. With gut certainty I knew he'd gone to see Gladys. If I was right it could be the break I needed. If I was wrong so what? No college wanted me anyway. Betting everything on Gladys, I wrote non-stop for another forty-five minutes. At a quarter to two I stopped. Put it on his desk and exited the building using the stairs instead of the elevator so I wouldn't run into him.* (Duffy exits.)

(Lights down on Carswell's office and up on the table bearing the Royal portable, where Duffy regards several letters.)

DUFFY: *I felt pumped up. Then I got home and found more turndowns. (Dropping each letter in a waste basket as he names the source.) Seton Hall...Manhattan...Fordham...And a place I didn't even remember applying to. Rejections 18, acceptances zero. But it was still a great summer: Someone getting discharged every week made it a continuous party.* "You're never going to know how much a hundred dollars is worth until you try to borrow it," *my father said. By the end of July, my crap game winnings all but gone, I was thinking about getting a job when I came home at noon one Saturday and found my mother in tears.*

(Lights down on Duffy and up on his mother weeping as Duffy appears.)

DUFFY: What's the matter?

(She can't speak. He assumes another family row.)

DUFFY: What did he do *this* time?

(She shakes her head decisively.)

DUFFY: You didn't have a fight?

(She nods.)

DUFFY: What then?...Ma what is it?

(Too emotional to speak, she hands him an opened envelope which he regards.)

DUFFY: It's from Dartmouth.

(She nods. He explores the envelope finds it empty.)

DUFFY: Where's the letter?

MRS. DUFFY: Your father...

DUFFY: He opened my mail?

(She nods.)

DUFFY: Where is it?

MRS. DUFFY: He took it.

DUFFY: Took it where?

MRS. DUFFY: Out.

DUFFY: He went out with my letter?

(Mrs Duffy nods.)

DUFFY: Why?

MRS. DUFFY: *(Barely able to get it out.)* They want you.

DUFFY: Who wants me?

MRS. DUFFY: Dartmouth.

(Lights down on Mrs Duffy weeping anew.)

DUFFY: *I caught up to my father at the Park Plaza Bar and Grill where he was showing the letter to everyone, buying drinks and leading toasts to Dartmouth. My first reaction was I'm dreaming. Then I read the letter. "It's a mistake," I thought. "An error they'll correct." But it wasn't a mistake. The door to heaven had opened and I was in. My first day at Dartmouth I was walking down the street when lo and behold—the frosting on the cake!*

(Lights up on Captain Whitley in civilian dress as Duffy approaches him.)

DUFFY: Captain Whitley I presume.

(Whitley turns.)

DUFFY: Remember me?

WHITLEY: *(Astonished.)* It can't be.

DUFFY: It is.

WHITLEY: What are you doing here?

DUFFY: I'm a member of the Class of 1950.

WHITLEY: *(Scornfully.)* They must be letting anybody in.

(Lights down on Whitley.)

DUFFY: I resisted the urge to hit him—the look on his face punishment enough. Dean Strong, Professor Jensen, the Dexter brothers, Acting Dean Chamberlin, and last but not least, Gladys, I thank you all…Sixteen years after I graduated from Dartmouth I returned to receive an honorary degree. But that's another story.

(Lights down.)

THE END

THE VIEWING

INTRODUCTION

I spent the seven years after Dartmouth (and one year at Yale Drama) totally absorbed with the need to make a living: jazz band (trumpet); advertising (never got out of the messenger room at Young & Rubicam); subsistence gambler (one whose goal is a living not a killing); beach cabana salesman.

And all the while trying to get a toehold in live television. "The Golden Age" when all was written on spec for chicken feed.

Which left no time for plays.

Circa 1957 I'd written enough TV to make a brief return to my first love. *The Viewing* is the result.

It was produced, in house, at the Actor's Studio some years later.

The cast (over twenty roles—all male) allowed a lot of young turks to strut their stuff. Several rose to prominence, Harvey Keitel remembered most vividly.

Size of cast making commercial production impossible, I filed it away intending to make a movie of it, which so far I've not gotten around to.

Not that it matters (life no excuse for art), but except for the ending, it derives from personal experience.

I never did go to see that body. I'm not sure why.

SCENE I

Time: March, 1945. Place: A deserted German village in the wake of recent fighting. It is a clear full-moon night. Three areas command attention: A bare rectangular room; A smaller room, in another house, containing a table and two chairs; A clearing on a wooded rise behind the town. Moonlight touches the rooms so they are not altogether dark and probes the clearing like a spotlight. Vehicles are pulling up nearby: One, another, another, another, another. As they come to a halt their engines are silenced. Now the last one is quiet. We hear the jumbled mutterings of many men. Now an authoritative voice bawls over all.

VOICE: *(Offstage.)* Okay hold it.
   (There is immediate silence.)
VOICE: We're staying here overnight. First platoon gets that building with the arch way. Second takes the wooden one over there. Third platoon gets that garage or whatever it is. Headquarters takes the one behind me. Fall out.
   (There is the sound of the men moving off to their billets. After a few moments the Sergeant appears in the doorway of the larger room, sweeps it with a flashlight, then calls back to others outside.)
SERGEANT: All right. My section in here.
   (Nine men enter the room. The Second Soldier stumbles bumping into the Fourth.)
FOURTH SOLDIER: Watch out where you're going.
SECOND SOLDIER: Pardon me.
THIRD SOLDIER: Nice and cozy, huh?
   (They select places around the room and drop their bedrolls and gear.)
REVERE: Looks like it might have been a dining room.
SIXTH SOLDIER: Who's got candles?
SERGEANT: No lights tonight.
SIXTH SOLDIER: I want to write a letter.
FIRST SOLDIER: Me too. We'll black out the windows.
SERGEANT: No lights.
WEBB: Whose order is that?
SERGEANT: Mine.
SIXTH SOLDIER: How come?
SERGEANT: I'm tired. I want to get some sleep.
REVERE: What about us? Don't we have any rights?
   (Several of the others grumble similar sentiments.)

SERGEANT: *(Wearily, mechanically.)* I'll repeat my standing offer. Anybody don't want to do what I tell them just has to say so and we'll settle it out back. You lick me I'll turn in my stripes and recommend you get them. Anybody want to take that offer?

(He waits. No answer.)

SERGEANT: Okay then, it's no lights.

(The men mutter disgruntledly, spread out their bed rolls and climb into them.)

FIFTH SOLDIER: What's the name of this town?

SECOND SOLDIER: Who knows?

THIRD SOLDIER: Who cares?

FIFTH SOLDIER: It's the first German town we ever stayed at. In years to come it might be nice if you could pick it out on a map.

SECOND SOLDIER: Why?

THIRD SOLDIER: So he can bore his children.

REVERE: How far you figure we are from the front?

FOURTH SOLDIER: Can't be too far.

FIRST SOLDIER: Finley said the Germans pulled out of here yesterday morning.

FOURTH SOLDIER: I think we'll see action tomorrow.

(Gradually they are dropping off to sleep.)

WEBB: You been saying that every night for four days.

FIFTH SOLDIER: I wonder where the people who lived here are.

REVERE: Yeah, it's like a ghost town.

THIRD SOLDIER: *(To the Second Soldier, good-naturedly.)* Hey Keller, you think your wife is getting much these days?

SIXTH SOLDIER: Not much but regular.

(There is some laughter.)

FIRST SOLDIER: *(To the Second who is sleeping next to him.)* I bet there's some souvenirs around.

SECOND SOLDIER: You think so?

FIRST SOLDIER: Sure, they must have left something.

SECOND SOLDIER: Want to take a look in the morning?

FIRST SOLDIER: Yeah.

SERGEANT: *(Half asleep.)* Knock it off.

FIRST SOLDIER: *(More quietly.)* We'll go fifty-fifty on everything we find. Okay?

SECOND SOLDIER: Okay.

(A candle is lit in the other room, revealing the Captain and his Orderly. The Orderly deposits the candle on the table, drapes a blanket over the win-

dow, lights another candle, arranges the Captain's bedroll on the floor, then hangs a map on the wall. While he does these things the Captain sits at the table in an attitude of preoccupation.)

ORDERLY: Will you want the checker board. sir?

CAPTAIN: No, not tonight.

ORDERLY: I'll leave it out in case you change your mind. *(He takes a checker board and checkers from the Captain's pack and places it on top of his gear.)* You look tired, sir.

CAPTAIN: I guess everyone is.

ORDERLY: Yes sir, but I think it's a little harder on them that have the responsibility. Good night, sir.

(He goes out as the Exec Officer, a first Lieutenant, enters, a letter in his hand.)

CAPTAIN: *(To the Exec.)* Everything all right?

EXEC: Far as I know. *(Holds out the letter pleasurefully.)* Get a load of this.

CAPTAIN: *(Suspiciously.)* What is it?

EXEC: A letter from Karowski to his wife telling what he's going to do to her when he gets home…

(The Captain makes no move to accept the letter.)

EXEC: Evidently she's been sleeping with a friend of his and describing it to him in detail. Trying to drive him nuts, I guess. Read his reply. It's classic.

(The Captain hesitates a moment and then against his will takes the letter and reads to himself. He doesn't go too far before he puts it down.)

CAPTAIN: It's disgusting.

EXEC: That's putting it mildly. *(Picks up the letter and re-reads part of it to himself.)* I think the boy has real talent. Take this part where he vows to put red paint all over her—

CAPTAIN: *(Adamantly.)* —I don't want to hear it…You intend to pass that letter?

EXEC: It doesn't contain any military secrets as far as I can see.

CAPTAIN: Why do you insist on bringing these things to my attention?

EXEC: My apologies…You know, you ought to censor the mail sometime. It's a broadening experience.

(There is the sound of artillery; they both listen.)

EXEC: Sounds a lot closer than it was last night.

CAPTAIN: Yes.

EXEC: Guess we'll be in the soup tomorrow for sure…Good night.

CAPTAIN: Good night.

(The Exec goes out. The Captain blows out the candles, then takes the blanket from the window and stands there looking out as the artillery goes on intermittently. In the other room.)

FIRST SOLDIER: *(Tentatively.)* You still awake, Keller?

SECOND SOLDIER: *(Drowsily.)* Yeah.

FIRST SOLDIER: You hear that artillery?

SECOND SOLDIER: Yeah.

FIRST SOLDIER: Sounds pretty near, huh?

(No answer.)

FIRST SOLDIER: Suppose we find only one souvenir tomorrow?

SECOND SOLDIER: We'll chose for it.

(The artillery sounds.)

FIRST SOLDIER: I wonder who's catching that stuff.

(Then silence. After a few moments the Sergeant rises.)

FIRST SOLDIER: That you, Sarge?

SERGEANT: Yes.

FIRST SOLDIER: You hear that artillery?

(The Sergeant starts from the room.)

FIRST SOLDIER: Where you going?

(The Sergeant exits.)

FIRST SOLDIER: You awake, Keller?

(No answer.)

FIRST SOLDIER: Anyone awake?

(No answer. The Sergeant appears at the clearing, is walking through it, then stops abruptly, looks at the ground and remains looking as the moon is hidden by a cloud and everything is blacked out.)

SCENE II

Time: The following morning. At rise: Clear and sunny. The Captain is playing checkers with the Exec Officer. The Fourth, Fifth, Sixth, Seventh Soldiers, Webb, Revere and the Sergeant are in the other room writing letters, fixing gear, resting. The First and Second Soldiers appear at the edge of the clearing.

FIRST SOLDIER: *(Nervously.)* We better not go much further.

SECOND SOLDIER: Why?

FIRST SOLDIER: They're liable to take off without us.

SECOND SOLDIER: Quit worrying, we ain't gone more than a hundred yards.

FIRST SOLDIER: We won't find anything anyway.

SECOND SOLDIER: Eastman found a canteen back of their billet.

FIRST SOLDIER: Some souvenir.

SECOND SOLDIER: Germans were in this town two days ago. They must have left something behind. You said so yourself. I'm gonna look some more. Coming?

FIRST SOLDIER: No. I ain't that crazy for souvenirs. Besides, we'll have all of them we want soon's we get into combat.

SECOND SOLDIER: Well, I'm gonna look some more.

FIRST SOLDIER: See you later...You better not go too far.

(The First Soldier turns back. The Second starts across the clearing, then stops, looks down, then without turning.)

SECOND SOLDIER: *(Excitedly.)* Hey...Hey, come on back.

FIRST SOLDIER: What is it?

(No answer.)

FIRST SOLDIER: What is it?

SECOND SOLDIER: A dead German.

(The First Soldier comes to the Second's side.)

FIRST SOLDIER: *(After staring a moment.)* I guess we're the first in the whole outfit to see one. Probably in the whole division.

SECOND SOLDIER: Yeah.

FIRST SOLDIER: A corporal, ain't he?

SECOND SOLDIER: Yeah...I'll go tell the others. You wait here.

FIRST SOLDIER: All right...Hurry up.

(The Second leaves the clearing. In a little while two soldiers join the First to view the body and soon there is a steady turnover of viewers which continues throughout most of the play. The Third Soldier sticks his head in the doorway of the larger room.)

THIRD SOLDIER: There's a dead German soldier back of where second platoon is. *(He disappears.)*

FOURTH SOLDIER: *(To the Fifth.)* Want to take a look?

FIFTH SOLDIER: Okay.

(They get up and go out.)

SIXTH SOLDIER: Think I'll go too. *(Rises, turns to the Sergeant.)* You coming?

SERGEANT: I already seen it.

SIXTH SOLDIER: *(Mildly surprised.)* You didn't say nothing.

SERGEANT: *(Irritated.)* It's just a guy lying there dead. What's to say?

SIXTH SOLDIER: *(Accepts this.)* Yeah, I guess so. *(He goes off.)*

PRIVATE WEBB: *(To Private Revere.)* Think I'll go take a look. You coming, Revere?

REVERE: No.

WEBB: Why not?

REVERE: I don't feel like it.

WEBB: I'll bet you never seen a dead person.

REVERE: I saw one before you. When I was eight years old.

WEBB: I'll bet you did.

REVERE: I did.

(Webb goes out. Revere turns to the Seventh Soldier lying next to him, who has been absently listening to the conversation.)

REVERE: It was a boy that lived on my block. He was laid out at home...I did it on a dare.

(The Seventh Soldier just looks at him disinterestedly and Revere turns away and busies himself. Lieutenant Finley enters the Captain's billet.)

FINLEY: Captain.

CAPTAIN: *(Looks up from the checker board.)* What is it?

FINLEY: Couple of the men found a dead German near the second platoon billet. He's attracting quite an audience. Thought you might be interested. *(He goes out.)*

EXEC: *(To the Captain.)* Let's go take a look. *(Rises.)*

CAPTAIN: You think that's wise?

EXEC: What do you mean?

CAPTAIN: I mean I think it will look a little silly if the Captain and the Executive Officer go up there and gawk like all the others.

EXEC: I'm not going to gawk. I'm just going to take a look. I never saw a dead soldier.

CAPTAIN: I don't think it's smart.

EXEC: Why?

CAPTAIN: It would show the men you had no more control over your morbid curiosity than they do.

EXEC: *(Sits down.)* You're the boss. *(Ends the checker game with a triple jump.)*

CAPTAIN: Well, that's fifteen I owe you. Want to play another?

EXEC: Not right now. I think I'll get some air. See you later. *(He exits.)*

CAPTAIN: *(Calls after him.)* Ask Finley if he wants to play.

(At the clearing. Among the audience about the body are the First, Third, Fourth, Fifth, Sixth, Eighth and Ninth Soldiers. Webb appears.)

THIRD SOLDIER: What's that insignia there?

FIRST SOLDIER: Infantry.

(Silence.)

THIRD SOLDIER: I'll bet those boots he has on are a lot warmer than ours.

FIRST SOLDIER: Me and Keller found him.

FOURTH SOLDIER: How old you figure he is?

SIXTH SOLDIER: Twenty, twenty-one.

WEBB: I don't think he's more than nineteen.

THIRD SOLDIER: Me neither…I wonder how long he's dead?

FIRST SOLDIER: Rigor mortis set in.

THIRD SOLDIER: How long's that take?

FIRST SOLDIER: I'm not sure.

FIFTH SOLDIER: *(With authority.)* He can't be dead too long.

(They turn to him.)

FIFTH SOLDIER: There's no smell.

(Silence.)

FOURTH SOLDIER: *(To the Fifth.)* I'm going back. You coming?

FIFTH SOLDIER: Not right away.

FOURTH SOLDIER: See you later.

FIFTH SOLDIER: Yeah.

(Fourth Soldier leaves.)

THIRD SOLDIER: I wonder how he got it.

FIRST SOLDIER: In the chest there. Don't you see the stain?

THIRD SOLDIER: I'm not blind. I meant I wondered what the circumstances were.

FIRST SOLDIER: Oh.

SIXTH SOLDIER: Could be he killed himself.

WEBB: Where's the gun?

SIXTH SOLDIER: Someone could have taken it.

FIRST SOLDIER: When me and Keller found him he didn't have a gun.

FIFTH SOLDIER: Maybe it's underneath him.

WEBB: *(Eagerly.)* Yeah.

FIRST SOLDIER: *(Hastily.)* No. No, it's not.

(The others turn to him.)

FIRST SOLDIER: Me and Keller looked.

FIFTH SOLDIER: *(Surprised.)* You turned him over?

FIRST SOLDIER: Yeah.

THIRD SOLDIER: How did you know he wasn't booby trapped?

FIRST SOLDIER: I never thought about it.

FIFTH SOLDIER: *(Looks at the body again.)* He didn't bleed much.

WEBB: What's that prove?

FIFTH SOLDIER: I was just noticing.

(*Tenth and Eleventh Soldiers join the circle.*)

TENTH SOLDIER: (*After looking a moment.*) He's a kid.

ELEVENTH SOLDIER: Yeah.

THIRD SOLDIER: (*To the Tenth.*) Any word about when we're pulling out?

TENTH SOLDIER: Not yet.

THIRD SOLDIER: Wonder what's holding us up?

TENTH SOLDIER: I don't know, but the old man got a message from Division in the middle of the night.

THIRD SOLDIER: New orders?

TENTH SOLDIER: Search me. How long you figure he's dead?

FIRST SOLDIER: Long enough for rigor mortis.

ELEVENTH SOLDIER: How long's that?

FIRST SOLDIER: I don't know…I bet a medic would know.

THIRD SOLDIER: Don't it give you the creeps the way he's staring?

FIFTH SOLDIER: Yeah.

TENTH SOLDIER: It gives *me* the creeps the way *we're* staring.

FIRST SOLDIER: Me and Keller found him. We were out looking for souvenirs.

TENTH SOLDIER: (*To First Soldier.*) What are you gonna do, saw him in half? (*He turns and goes off. The Eleventh Soldier goes after him.*)

FIRST SOLDIER: (*Looks after the Tenth.*) What's wrong with *him?*

WEBB: I guess corpses upset him. Some guys are like that. Take Revere. You couldn't get Revere up here to see this with a bull dozer.

EIGHTH SOLDIER: The same with a couple of guys in my platoon.

THIRD SOLDIER: What'll they do when we go into combat. You can't fight with your eyes closed.

NINTH SOLDIER: I guess it takes something like this to separate the men from the boys.

(*The Executive Officer enters the circle.*)

EXEC: Good morning, fellows.

THE MEN: (*Jovially.*) Hi, Lieutenant.

EXEC: (*Looking down.*) Not very pretty, is it?

SIXTH SOLDIER: No sir.

FIRST SOLDIER: (*To the Exec.*) The captain know about it?

EXEC: Yes.

FIRST SOLDIER: He coming up to see it?

EXEC: No.

FIRST SOLDIER: Why not?

EXEC: He's too busy.

THIRD SOLDIER: Playing checkers?

(They all laugh including the Exec. Officer.)

WEBB: You know, Lieutenant, some guys won't come up here because they've got weak stomachs. You sure that isn't what's keeping the old man away?

EXEC: I refuse to answer on the grounds it might incriminate me.

(They all laugh. He looks at the body.)

EXEC: Anybody check to see if he's booby trapped?

THIRD SOLDIER: *(Indicating the First Soldier.)* Yeah. This putz and Keller turned him over looking for souvenirs.

EXEC: *(To the First Soldier.)* That was pretty dumb, wasn't it?

FIRST SOLDIER: *(Embarrassed.)* Yes sir. I...We didn't consider he might be trapped.

EXEC: Next time use a rope, a long rope, and pull him.

FIRST SOLDIER: Yes sir.

EXEC: Well, back to the checker board. See you men. *(Starts off.)*

THIRD SOLDIER: How much you take from him today?

EXEC: *(Calls back.)* A hundred and twenty so far.

(They laugh.)

THIRD SOLDIER: *(Looking after the Exec.)* They don't come more regular than him.

FIFTH SOLDIER: Too bad he ain't CO.

(The Twelfth Soldier joins the circle. He looks down and unconsciously removes his helmet in token of reverence. The others turn to him curiously. He doesn't understand at first and then follows their eyes to his helmet.)

TWELFTH SOLDIER: *(Embarrassed as he puts the helmet back on his head.)* I forgot where I was. *(Looks at the body.)* How old you figure he is?

(In the large room, the Fourth and Seventh Soldiers, the Sergeant and Revere are present.)

SEVENTH SOLDIER: *(To the Fourth.)* How old is he?

FOURTH SOLDIER: Eighteen or nineteen. Twenty at the most.

SERGEANT: *(With quiet assurance.)* He's close to thirty.

FOURTH SOLDIER: Who told you that?

SERGEANT: I saw him.

FOURTH SOLDIER: Gee, I don't see how you figure thirty.

(The Sergeant doesn't reply, ending the conversation. The Fourth Soldiers turns back to the Seventh.)

FOURTH SOLDIER: You going up to take a look?

SEVENTH SOLDIER: No.

FOURTH SOLDIER: Seen enough like him, huh?

SEVENTH SOLDIER: That's right.

REVERE: *(To the Fourth.)* Many guys there?

FOURTH SOLDIER: Yeah. *(To the Seventh Soldier.)* I guess you'd rather be going into action with your old outfit than a green bunch like us.

SEVENTH SOLDIER: Why?

FOURTH SOLDIER: I don't know, I just thought you would.

REVERE: *(To the Fourth Soldier.)* How did he get killed?

FOURTH SOLDIER: Bullet in the chest. *(Points to his own chest.)* Right here. *(Turns to Seventh Soldier.)* I guess there ain't many of the original guys left of your old outfit, huh?

SEVENTH SOLDIER: No.

FOURTH SOLDIER: How many left in your company when you got hit?

SEVENTH SOLDIER: Forty.

REVERE: *(To the Fourth Soldier.)* He's just laying there, huh?

FOURTH SOLDIER: Yeah, right in the middle of this clearing. On his back. Staring at the sky.

REVERE: Infantry?

FOURTH SOLDIER: Yeah.

REVERE: Enlisted man?

SERGEANT: *(Irritated, to Revere.)* For crying out loud, if you're that interested, go up and see for yourself.

FOURTH SOLDIER: *(To the Seventh.)* Any word about pulling out?

SEVENTH SOLDIER: No.

REVERE: It's almost noon. What do you suppose is keeping us here?

FOURTH SOLDIER: The Captain got new orders from Division in the middle of the night. That could have something to do with it.

SERGEANT: Where'd you hear that?

FOURTH SOLDIER: Up at the clearing. From a headquarters guy.

REVERE: Could be that rumor is true.

FOURTH SOLDIER: What rumor's that?

REVERE: The one about us going to guard prisoners.

FOURTH SOLDIER: I never heard that one.

REVERE: It was going around the other day. Maybe we're waiting for a load of prisoners right now.

FOURTH SOLDIER: Boy, wouldn't that be the nuts: guarding prisoners.

(The Thirteenth Soldier enters the room and calls to the Fourth.)

THIRTEENTH SOLDIER: Hey Boley, you see that German they found?

FOURTH SOLDIER: Yeah. You?

THIRTEENTH SOLDIER: I'm on my way now. Wanna come?

FOURTH SOLDIER: Okay.

REVERE: *(Reproachfully.)* You already seen it once.

FOURTH SOLDIER: So what? *(Starts out.)*

SERGEANT: *(To the Fourth Soldier as he passes.)* Did you notice anything about him?

FOURTH SOLDIER: About the German?

SERGEANT: Yes.

FOURTH SOLDIER: Like what?

(The Sergeant looks off without answering.)

THIRTEENTH SOLDIER: *(Impatiently.)* Come on, Boley.

FOURTH SOLDIER: *(Turns away from the Sergeant with a slight look of puzzlement which disappears almost immediately.)* Take your time. He ain't gonna run away. *(He goes out with the Thirteenth Soldier.)*

REVERE: *(Self-righteously.)* I guess there must be something wrong with me. I don't want to see it at all. *(To the Seventh Soldier.)* What do you think of this outfit?

SEVENTH SOLDIER: I've only been in it a week.

REVERE: You must have got some impressions. *(Pulls a candy bar from his belongings, extends it to the Seventh Soldier.)* Have a candy bar.

(The Seventh Soldier wants it, but hesitates.)

REVERE: *(Continued.)* Go ahead. I'm trying to clear up my complexion.

(The Seventh Soldier accepts it, aware that it obligates him to continue the conversation.)

SEVENTH SOLDIER: Thanks.

REVERE: Don't mention it...You think there's any way of predicting beforehand which guys are going to get killed?

SEVENTH SOLDIER: I never thought about it. *(Now a thought hits him.)* I'll tell you something though. There was this one fellow I owed some money to. The night before we first went into action he told me to forget it. I argued with him but it didn't do no good. It was like he'd just suddenly lost interest in money altogether. Turned out he was one of the first guys we lost.

SERGEANT: *(Peevishly.)* What's that prove?

SEVENTH SOLDIER: I don't know. *(Turns to Revere.)* What you were saying reminded me of it.

REVERE: You think he had a premonition he was going to die?

SEVENTH SOLDIER: I don't know.

REVERE: Makes you stop and wonder, don't it…Take a guy like Shellburne in the second platoon: He's the bald corporal. The heavy guy.

SEVENTH SOLDIER: What about him?

REVERE: He's the most decent guy I ever met. If the good die young he can't miss. Or take—

SERGEANT: *(Angrily.)* —Knock it off.

REVERE: Why?

SERGEANT: 'Cause I told you to.

REVERE: We were just talking.

SERGEANT: You were talking bull and I'm sick of listening to it.

REVERE: We got a right to talk about anything we want.

SERGEANT: *(Wearily.)* Oh, don't start in about your rights again or I'll come over there and dump you on your tail.

REVERE: Boy, you're sure getting touchy lately.

(This hits the Sergeant hard. He gets to his feet, walks to Revere and stands above him threateningly.)

SERGEANT: What do you mean by that?

REVERE: *(Frightened.)* Just that you seem out of sorts…That's all.

(The Sergeant looks at him a moment, then as though he'd just wakened to find himself in an embarrassing position, he turns somewhat sheepishly to the Seventh Soldier.)

SERGEANT: Got a cigarette?

SEVENTH SOLDIER: Yeah. *(Hands him one.)*

SERGEANT: Thanks. *(Returns to his place.)*

(They regard him. The Fifth and Sixth Soldiers enter.)

FIFTH SOLDIER: *(To Sixth.)* You think they'd let it go through if I mention it in a letter?

SIXTH SOLDIER: Why not?

SEVENTH SOLDIER: How's the wake going?

SIXTH SOLDIER: *(Sardonic.)* Excellent. No man could ask for a better turnout.

REVERE: *(To the Fifth Soldier.)* What did you do up there?

FIFTH SOLDIER: Just stand around. *(Turns.)* Anyone got writing paper handy?

SEVENTH SOLDIER: Yeah, here. *(Hands it to him.)*

FIFTH SOLDIER: Thanks.

(He sits on the floor, propped against the wall and starts to write. The Sixth Soldier flops down beside his belongings, digs out an unopened pint of whiskey, opens it. The Seventh Soldier, who is beside him, looks on.)

SEVENTH SOLDIER: *(To the Sixth.)* I thought you were saving that for a special occasion.

SIXTH SOLDIER: I did.

(He drinks from the bottle, then offers it to the Seventh Soldier who takes a drink and passes it back.)

SIXTH SOLDIER: Today it's come to my attention there's a war on. *(Drinks again.)*

FIFTH SOLDIER: *(Looks up from his letter and speaks to the Sixth Soldier.)* How big would you say that clearing is?

SIXTH SOLDIER: Seven or eight yards across. *(Turns to the Seventh Soldier.)* It's also come to my attention today that a man is a fool to wait for a special occasion. *(Drinks.)* I know this is old stuff to you but for me it was an illuminating experience all around. *(Offers the bottle.)*

SEVENTH SOLDIER: No thanks.

FIFTH SOLDIER: *(Again looks up from his letter to the Sixth Soldier.)* Corporal, wasn't he?

SIXTH SOLDIER: That's right. *(Then sarcastically.)* Color of hair, brown; of eyes, blue.

FIFTH SOLDIER: *(Oblivious to the sarcasm.)* I already got that.

(At the clearing, present among others are the First, Fourth, Twelfth, Thirteenth, Fourteenth, Fifteenth Soldiers and Webb. The Twelfth Soldier leaves.)

FIFTEENTH SOLDIER: Don't look like much of a superman, does he?

FOURTEENTH SOLDIER: They must be scraping the barrel.

(The Sixteenth Soldier makes his way into the circle, looks down.)

WEBB: *(To the Sixteenth.)* Any sign of us pulling out?

SIXTEENTH SOLDIER: No.

FOURTEENTH SOLDIER: *(To Webb.)* You look disappointed. Anxious to see action?

WEBB: I'm not afraid of it.

FIFTEENTH SOLDIER: Myself I figure every minute more we spend here is a minute less we'll have to spend up there. I'd be delighted to sit out the whole thing right here where we are.

FOURTH SOLDIER: *(To the Fourteenth.)* There's a good chance it'll work out that way.

(They all look at him.)

FOURTH SOLDIER: I heard those new orders the old man got is for us to wait here for a bunch of POWs that we're going to guard.

WEBB: Says who?

FOURTH SOLDIER: Somebody heard the first sergeant talking it over with Riley.

FIFTEENTH SOLDIER: That sure would be a nice break.

THIRTEENTH SOLDIER: *(To the Fourth.)* How could we guard them here? There's no stockade or anything.

FOURTH SOLDIER: I'm just telling you what I heard.

FIFTEENTH SOLDIER: Maybe we don't guard them here. Maybe we escort them back to the rear.

(A Medic, identified by the cross on his helmet, approaches the ring.)

MEDIC: All right, gentlemen, step aside. The old medicine man is on the scene. Make way there. *(Now he comes to the front line and the view of the corpse has an instantly arresting and sobering effect on him. He just stands looking.)*

FIRST SOLDIER: *(To the Medic.)* How long's it take for rigor mortis to set in?

MEDIC: How should I know.

FIRST SOLDIER: You're a medic, ain't you?

MEDIC: *(Without taking his eyes from the body.)* Yeah, but not an undertaker…Just a kid, ain't he?

FOURTEENTH SOLDIER: Yeah.

FIRST SOLDIER: Me and Keller found him.

(The Fourth and Thirteenth Soldiers leave. The Second Soldier enters the circle beside the First Soldier.)

SECOND SOLDIER: *(Triumphantly to the First.)* Look. *(He holds out a bayonet.)*

FIRST SOLDIER: *(Disdainfully.)* What's that?

SECOND SOLDIER: What do you mean what's that? It's a German bayonet.

FIRST SOLDIER: *(To hide his envy.)* It's all cracked and rusted.

WEBB: *(To the Second Soldier.)* Where'd you find it?

SECOND SOLDIER: In a ditch by the road we came in on.

FOURTEENTH SOLDIER: Let's see.

(The Second Soldier passes him the bayonet which now begins a journey around the circle.)

SECOND SOLDIER: *(To the First.)* I told you I'd find something.

SIXTEENTH SOLDIER: I wonder if it was ever used.

FIRST SOLDIER: *(To the Second.)* You gonna send that beat-up thing home?

SECOND SOLDIER: Sure. And so would you if it was yours.

FIFTEENTH SOLDIER: *(Examining the bayonet, he speaks to the Fourteenth Soldier.)* Can you picture yourself using one of these?

FOURTEENTH SOLDIER: No, but I guess I would if it was me or the other guy.

WEBB: *(Not unhappily.)* We might all be using them before the day's over.

MEDIC: *(To Webb bitterly.)* Nothing would please you better, would it?

WEBB: The idea don't make my knees shake if that's what you mean.

MEDIC: That isn't what I mean. *(He goes off.)*

(Webb angrily slams the fist of one hand against the palm of the other.)

WEBB: Someday I'm going to let that wise guy have it.

SIXTEENTH SOLDIER: *(Looking at the body.)* What's that insignia he's wearing?

FIRST SOLDIER: Infantry.

(The bayonet has now passed to Webb's hands.)

WEBB: *(To the Second Soldier.)* I'll give you a buck for it.

SECOND SOLDIER: No.

WEBB: Two bucks.

SECOND SOLDIER: I don't want to sell it.

WEBB: Five bucks.

SECOND SOLDIER: No. Let me have it... *(Then anxiously.)* Let me have it, Webb.

(Webb holds it a moment more as though debating whether to give it back, then abrupt]y returns it.)

WEBB: Here. I wouldn't give you a dime for the rotten thing.

(Lieutenant Finley enters the circle and looks down.)

FOURTEENTH SOLDIER: How you think it happened, Lieutenant?

FINLEY: I don't know. A lot of them are deserting. Could be *he* tried, got caught, and they shot him.

FIFTEENTH SOLDIER: Why do you say that?

FINLEY: The way he was shot. Plus the fact he's not armed.

WEBB: *(To the Lieutenant.)* You know, Lieutenant, all the officers have been up here except the old man.

FINLEY: What's that supposed to mean?

WEBB: *(Impudently.)* Nothing, sir, I was just stating a fact.

(Several of the men laugh.)

FINLEY: *(Uncomfortable and anxious to change the subject, looks at the body.)* Who found him?

FIRST SOLDIER: *(Indicating the Second Soldier.)* Me and Keller here.

SECOND SOLDIER: *(Indignantly.)* What do you mean "me and Keller?" You were already going back when I called you to come see. *(To the Lieutenant.)* I found him all by myself.

FOURTEENTH SOLDIER: *(To the Second.)* Show him your souvenir.

SECOND SOLDIER: *(Holds up the bayonet.)* I found this too.

FINLEY: *(To the Second Soldier.)* You've had a busy day, haven't you? Let's see it.

(The bayonet is handed to him.)

FOURTEENTH SOLDIER: *(To the Lieutenant.)* How come we haven't pulled out yet?

FINLEY: *(As he turns the bayonet over in his hand.)* We're waiting for orders.

FIRST SOLDIER: We heard we're waiting for a load of prisoners and that we're going to guard them.

FINLEY: Who started that one? *(Hands the bayonet back.)* Here. *(He goes off.)*

SIXTEENTH SOLDIER: *(Significantly.)* You notice he didn't deny it, about the prisoners.

FOURTEENTH SOLDIER: *(Thoughtfully.)* Yeah.

FIFTEENTH SOLDIER: *(To Webb.)* Why you making such a big deal out of it that the Captain ain't been up here?

WEBB: Because I want to.

(The Seventeenth Soldier joins the circle. At the Captain's billet. The Exec and the Captain are again playing checkers. Lieutenant Finley enters.)

CAPTAIN: *(Indicating a pot over a can of Sterno.)* Help yourself to some coffee.

FINLEY: Thanks. *(Pours a cup.)*

CAPTAIN: *(To the Exec as they conclude a game.)* That's one for me. Brings it down to twelve.

(They set up the pieces of another game.)

FINLEY: I just saw that German they found.

(The Captain turns to him interestedly.)

CAPTAIN: *(Slightly sarcastic.)* Anything worth seeing?

FINLEY: Not especially.

CAPTAIN: What's his rank?

FINLEY: Corporal.

EXEC: It's your move, Captain.

(The Captain turns to the board and moves. The Exec moves. The Captain moves.)

CAPTAIN: *(To Finley without turning to him.)* How old?

FINLEY: Not more than twenty.

(The Exec moves.)

CAPTAIN: *(As he contemplates his move.)* Lot of the men up there?

FINLEY: Yes. I guess most of the company has seen it by now…You thinking of taking a look?

CAPTAIN: No.

FINLEY: Why?

CAPTAIN: *(Turns to him.)* Why do you ask?

FINLEY: Because when I was up at the clearing the men seemed to attach some significance to the fact that all the officers have seen the body except you.

CAPTAIN: How do you mean "attach some significance?"

FINLEY: They laughed about it.

CAPTAIN: Why?

FINLEY: I don't know.

EXEC: I think I do.

(They turn to him.)

EXEC: For some reason they think you're afraid.

CAPTAIN: *(Incredulously.)* Afraid to look at a dead man?

EXEC: Yes.

CAPTAIN: That's ridiculous.

EXEC: I know. That's why I didn't mention it to you.

CAPTAIN: *(Surprised.)* You heard them laugh at me? You were up there?

EXEC: Yes sir. I wanted to make sure the body had been checked for booby traps.

CAPTAIN: *(Not having thought of this himself, his anger is temporarily suspended in favor of curiosity.)* Was it?

EXEC: Yes sir.

CAPTAIN: I see. *(Now his previous indignation claims him. He turns to Finley.)* It's behind the second platoon billet?

FINLEY: Yes sir, about sixty yards along the trail. It's—

CAPTAIN: —I'll find it. *(To the Exec.)* You come with me. *(Goes out.)*

(At the clearing. Present are the First, Second, Fourteenth, Fifteenth, Sixteenth, Seventeenth Soldiers and Webb. The Seventeenth Soldier is examining the bayonet.)

SEVENTEENTH SOLDIER: It sure is an ugly looking thing.

(He passes it back to the Second Soldier. Now the First Soldier sees the Captain and the Executive Officer approach.)

FIRST SOLDIER: *(Snaps to attention.)* Tensh—hut.

(The other men all come to attention. The Captain and the Exec enter the circle.)

CAPTAIN: *(Looks around at their faces for a moment, then releases them.)* As you were.

(They resume their previous poses. He looks down at the body. After a moment, he speaks to the Exec without looking at him.)

CAPTAIN: That's a very sad sight.

EXEC: Yes sir.

(The Captain looks a moment more, then looks up at the First Soldier.)

CAPTAIN: How long you been here?

FIRST SOLDIER: Sir?

CAPTAIN: *(Harshly.)* How long have you been standing here like this?

FIRST SOLDIER: About an hour, sir.

CAPTAIN: You think that proves something? You think it indicates you're stronger than someone who had the decency to never come up here at all?

FIRST SOLDIER: *(Bewildered.)* No sir.

CAPTAIN: You're damn right it don't. All it shows is that you're a ghoul. *(Looks around at the others.)* I guess you all know what a ghoul is. Huh? *(Now the Captain contemplates the body again. After a moment he voices a thought.)* I wonder if we should bury him.

EXEC: *(Alertly.)* I don't believe it's necessary, sir. There are special units for that.

CAPTAIN: *(Shortly.)* Don't you think I know that?

EXEC: *(Contritely.)* Yes sir.

(Feeling that his authority has been compromised by this last exchange and that the men are taking amusement in it, the Captain looks around maliciously.)

CAPTAIN: *(Indicating the body.)* You'll be seeing a lot like him before very long. And they won't all be Germans.

(He goes off abruptly. The Exec follows him.)

SEVENTEENTH SOLDIER: *(Puzzled.)* What the devil was that all about?

(At the Soldiers' Billet, where a crap game involving the Third, Fourth, Seventh, Eighth, Eleventh and Thirteenth Soldiers is in progress. The Sergeant, his head on his bed roll, lies on the floor looking at the ceiling. The Fifth Soldier is still composing his letter. The Sixth Soldier is nursing his pint of whiskey. Revere is cleaning his rifle. The Thirteenth Soldier throws the dice.)

THIRD SOLDIER: Up jumped the devil.

(The Thirteenth Soldier has sevened out. The faders collect their money which is in Army Script.)

THIRD SOLDIER: Next shooter.

(The Fourth Soldier takes the dice.)

FOURTH SOLDIER: *(Dropping several bills on the floor.)* Shoot thirty.

THIRD SOLDIER: *(Puts a bill down.)* I got ten of it.

SEVENTH SOLDIER: *(Puts a bill down.)* I'll take five.

THIRTEENTH SOLDIER: *(Puts a bill down.)* I'll take the rest.

(The Fourth Soldier throws the dice.)

THIRD SOLDIER: Tens the point.

SEVENTH SOLDIER: *(To the Fourth.)* Two to one no ten.

FOURTH SOLDIER: *(Dropping another bill.)* Five says I do.

(The Seventh Soldier covers the bet. The Fourth Soldier shakes the dice.)

FOURTH SOLDIER: Ten right back. *(He throws.)*

THIRD SOLDIER: Seven you lose.

(The faders gather their winnings.)

FIFTH SOLDIER: *(His letter finished, has been reading it over. Now he speaks to the fellows in the crap game.)* How big would you say that German is?

SIXTH SOLDIER: *(Sarcastically to the Fifth.)* You writing a book about him?

FIFTH SOLDIER: No. I just like to be accurate. *(To the crap shooters.)* How tall would you say?

THIRD SOLDIER: Five ten or eleven.

FIFTH SOLDIER: Yeah, that's what I put down.

EIGHTH SOLDIER: *(To the Third.)* What do you mean five ten or eleven? That guy ain't over five four. *(To the Thirteenth.)* You think he's over five four?

THIRTEENTH SOLDIER: No.

THIRD SOLDIER: *(To the Eighth.)* You're blind. Either that or we ain't talking about the same guy. *(To the Seventh.)* What do you say?

SEVENTH SOLDIER: I didn't see him.

ELEVENTH SOLDIER: *(Looking at the Eighth Soldier.)* I did and I think he's closer to five ten than he is to what you said.

FIFTH SOLDIER: So do I.

EIGHTH SOLDIER: I got twenty bucks says he ain't over five four. Put up or shut up.

THIRD SOLDIER: You're on. Anyone else say he's not over five four.

THIRTEENTH SOLDIER: I do.

THIRD SOLDIER: For how much?

THIRTEENTH SOLDIER: As much as you want?

THIRD SOLDIER: Twenty bucks.

THIRTEENTH SOLDIER: It's a bet.

ELEVENTH SOLDIER: *(To the Thirteenth.)* Ten more says he's more than five four.

THIRTEENTH SOLDIER: You got a bet. *(Looks around.)* Anyone else?

FIFTH SOLDIER: I'll bet you ten dollars.

THIRTEENTH SOLDIER: You're on.

THIRD SOLDIER: *(Rising.)* Come on.

(The Third, Fifth, Eighth, Eleventh and Thirteenth Soldiers go out. The Seventh and Fourth Soldiers drop down beside their gear.)

REVERE: *(To the Fourth Soldier.)* How come you didn't bet?

FOURTH SOLDIER: I'm broke.

SIXTH SOLDIER: *(Who is quite drunk, reaches over and picks up the letter the Fifth Soldier was writing. He reads a bit of it to himself, then laughs unpleasantly. The others look at him.)* Get this. It's Balch's letter to his girl. *(He reads from the letter.)* "Dearest Love—"

FOURTH SOLDIER: *(To the Sixth.)* —I don't think you should do that.

SIXTH SOLDIER: Why not?

FOURTH SOLDIER: It's not right.

SIXTH SOLDIER: But it *is* right to bet on the height of a corpse?

FOURTH SOLDIER: Ah, you're drunk. *(He looks away.)*

SIXTH SOLDIER: *(Resumes reading from the letter.)* "Dearest Love, Today we came across a dead German soldier who was killed in action and wasn't buried. I guess that means we are really getting near to the real fighting. I did not want to go see the body but I forced myself because I think it is better to harden one's self to these things in view of what is probably in store for us. He is lying in a clearing eight yards wide and staring at the sky. He is just a boy, probably younger than me with brown hair and blue eyes. You can plainly see where the bullet hit. Some of the—

SERGEANT: *(Shouts.)* —Knock it off.

(The intensity with which he says this cuts through the Sixth Soldier's jag.)

SIXTH SOLDIER: *(After a moment's hesitation.)* Okay, Sarge, but just let me tell you how it ends. After running on for two pages about our corpse he says: "I surely hope all this doesn't upset you." Signed "All my love and a million kisses, Arnold." *(Looks around, holding up the letter.)* Now is that a love letter or is that a love letter. *(He drops the letter where it was and spent, flops back in his original place on the floor.)*

(The Sergeant leans over and speaks privately to the Fourth Soldier.)

SERGEANT: Did you notice anything about the German the second time you saw him?

FOURTH SOLDIER: No.

SERGEANT: Did you look hard?

FOURTH SOLDIER: *(Uncomfortable.)* Yeah.

SERGEANT: And you didn't notice anything?

FOURTH SOLDIER: No. No, I didn't.

SERGEANT: *(Desperately.)* You wouldn't kid me, would you?

FOURTH SOLDIER: *(Almost frightened.)* No.

(The Sergeant lies back and resumes looking at the ceiling while the Fourth Soldier eyes him curiously. Now the Fourth Soldier speaks to him.)

FOURTH SOLDIER: Sarge, what is it? What did you *expect* me to notice?

SERGEANT: *(With matter-of-fact certainty.)* He looks like me.

(At the clearing, present are the First, Second, Third, Fifth, Eighth, Eleventh, Thirteenth, Fourteenth, Seventeenth Soldiers and Webb.)

EIGHTH SOLDIER: *(Looking down at the body as he folds up a yard stick.)* He sure didn't look six foot to me.

THIRD SOLDIER: That's because you didn't take into account he's dead.

THIRTEENTH SOLDIER: *(Peevishly.)* What's that got to do with it?

THIRD SOLDIER: You ever see a stage play?

THIRTEENTH SOLDIER: Yeah.

THIRD SOLDIER: Did you ever notice how the actors all seem much bigger than they are in real life?

THIRTEENTH SOLDIER: No.

FIFTH SOLDIER: I did.

EIGHTH SOLDIER: Me too. What about it?

THIRD SOLDIER: If a guy seems bigger than he really is when he's up on a stage moving around don't it figure he's gonna look smaller when he's laying down very still. *(To the Thirteenth.)* I'll take my twenty now... *(Turns to the Eighth.)* ...and twenty from you.

ELEVENTH SOLDIER: (To the Thirteenth.) Let's have the ten.

(The bets are paid off.)

FIFTH SOLDIER: Maybe we could pull the same bet on some other guys.

FOURTEENTH SOLDIER: *(Looking at the body.)* Do they wear dog tags like us?

SEVENTEENTH SOLDIER: I think so.

EIGHTH SOLDIER: *(To the Fourteenth.)* Why?

FOURTEENTH SOLDIER: We could learn something about him from his dog tags.

EIGHTH SOLDIER: *(To the Fourteenth, challengingly.)* Okay, go ahead. You fish out his dog tags and we'll take a look.

FOURTEENTH SOLDIER: *(Hastily.)* No thanks. I'm not that curious.

WEBB: *(Quietly but intense.)* I am.

(He hesitates a moment, then while they all watch he bends to the body and rises in a few moments, the dog tags in his hand.)

THIRD SOLDIER: *(To Webb.)* What's it say?

(Webb reads them but doesn't answer.)

THIRD SOLDIER: What's it say, Webb?

WEBB: *(Superiorly.)* Wouldn't you like to know?

THIRTEENTH SOLDIER: *(To Webb.)* Ain't you gonna tell us what it says?

WEBB: No. *(Turns to the Second Soldier.)* I guess this is one souvenir I beat you to. *(He starts away.)*

THIRD SOLDIER: Where you going? Hey, Webb.

(Webb goes off without answering. They all look after him.)

THIRTEENTH SOLDIER: *(Shocked.)* Who'd take a guy's dog tags for a souvenir?

FOURTEENTH SOLDIER: *He* would.

(At the Captain's Billet. The Captain sits at his table in troubled thought. Finley is looking at a map on the wall.)

FINLEY: This area is famous for wine.

(The Captain doesn't answer. Finley turns to him.)

FINLEY: The country around here is known for its wine.

CAPTAIN: Yes, I know…I wonder why they didn't bury him.

FINLEY: Probably pulled out too fast. I bet the first troops through here had a ball.

CAPTAIN: Why?

FINLEY: The wine. *(Watches the Captain a moment.)* Something on your mind?

CAPTAIN: The German…He should be buried. He shouldn't be left out there to rot.

FINLEY: I don't see that it matters.

(The Captain looks at him sharply.)

FINLEY: I mean he's dead. So what's the difference?

CAPTAIN: *(Angrily.)* The difference is that I don't think it's right.

FINLEY: Yes sir.

CAPTAIN: Deaths. Funerals. They're very important traditions where I come from…Very solemn. Very sacred.

FINLEY: They're like that where I live too, sir, but we're a long way from home.

CAPTAIN: *(Heatedly.)* Is that any reason for not doing the right thing when we have the chance?

FINLEY: Shall I arrange a detail?

CAPTAIN: No…The men would misunderstand. They'd think I was being soft.

FINLEY: Then we won't bury him.

CAPTAIN: No. But you can tell them the wake's over, that I don't want anyone else to go up there. It's indecent.

FINLEY: Yes sir. *(He exits.)*

(At the Soldier's Billet. Present are the Fourth, Sixth, Seventh Soldiers, Revere, the Sergeant and Webb.)

WEBB: *(To Revere.)* Just about everyone's been up there except you.

(Revere goes on cleaning his rifle, trying to ignore Webb.)

WEBB: Even the old man took a look…

(Revere doesn't speak.)

WEBB: You say you saw a stiff when you were eight.

REVERE: That's right.

WEBB: That the only one you ever saw?

REVERE: Yes.

WEBB: How did it affect you?

(Revere doesn't answer.)

WEBB: How did it affect you?

(Revere doesn't answer.)

WEBB: It must have had some effect on you.

REVERE: I was sick. *(Turns to Webb.)* It made me sick. You satisfied?

WEBB: What are you gonna do in combat: Fight with your eyes closed?

REVERE: I don't know what I'll do,

WEBB: *(Sarcastically.)* I can guess.

SEVENTH SOLDIER: Don't bet on it.

(Webb takes out the German's dog tags and begins to twirl them. He does this with the obvious purpose of attracting their attention. Aware of this, they try to ignore him. It is the Fourth Soldier who's curiosity gets the better of him.)

FOURTH SOLDIER: *(To Webb.)* What's that?

WEBB: What's it look like?

FOURTH SOLDIER: Dog tags…but different from ours.

WEBB: They're German… *(He gets their complete attention.)* I took them off our friend up there.

FOURTH SOLDIER: Why?

WEBB: I wanted a souvenir.

REVERE: You can't do that.

(Webb turns to him.)

REVERE: His people would never be able to find out he's dead. They'd keep hoping.

WEBB: So?

REVERE: So you can't do it.

WEBB: It's done.

REVERE: *(With quiet but zealous insistence.)* You've got to put them back.

(Reaches out for the tags. Webb brushes his hand aside.)

WEBB: Get away.

(Revere gets to his feet and with almost dream-like persistence, pursues the dog tags, reaching for them.)

WEBB: Beat it.

REVERE: *(Keeps coming on when Webb pushes him away.)* It's wrong, Webb. It's a terrible thing to do.

WEBB: *(To the others, indicating Revere whom he holds at arm's length.)* What's the matter with him?

REVERE: I want—

(He makes a sudden grab and Webb smacks him in the face. Revere falls back holding his face, looking dazedly at Webb.)

WEBB: I told you to lay off.

(He looks around at the others who are all staring at him coldly.)

WEBB: I warned him.

SIXTH SOLDIER: (To Webb, indicating Revere.) He's right. You've got to put them back.

WEBB: You gonna make me?

SIXTH SOLDIER: (Getting to his feet.) I'll try.

FOURTH SOLDIER: So will I.

SEVENTH SOLDIER: Me too.

SERGEANT: (From his place on the floor.) Put 'em back, Webb.

WEBB: (Defiantly.) No. (He takes a position with his back to the wall like a trapped animal.) Come on, let's see you make me.

(The Fourth, Sixth and Seventh Soldiers look at each other uncertainly, then by mutual consent they begin to inch toward Webb.)

SERGEANT: Wait.

(They stop. He rises and comes to Webb, stopping a few feet from him.)

SERGEANT: I want those tags. You gonna give them to me?

(Webb, afraid of the Sergeant, hesitates, wavers.)

WEBB: (Anxious to save face.) I'll make a deal…I'll turn them over, providing Revere is the one who goes up there and puts them back.

SERGEANT: (Ignores him.) You gonna give them to me?

(Webb hesitates another moment, then throws the tags on the floor.)

WEBB: (Furious at his defeat.) I wasn't gonna keep them anyway. (He goes out.)

SERGEANT: (Resuming his place on the floor.) Someone put them back.

(No one moves for a moment, then Revere bends down, takes the tags and goes out. At the clearing, present are the First, Second, Fifth, Eighth, Ninth and Thirteenth Soldiers. The Eighteenth Soldier joins the circle.)

EIGHTH SOLDIER: (To the Eighteenth.) Any sign of us pulling out?

EIGHTEENTH SOLDIER: (Regarding the body all the time he talks.) No. There's talk we're going to convoy some prisoners back to Paris. You guys hear anything about it?

FIFTH SOLDIER: Not the Paris part.

FIRST SOLDIER: (To the Eighteenth.) Where did you hear that?

EIGHTEENTH SOLDIER: Everyone's talking about it… (Then, indicating the body.) Wonder if he was ever in Paris?

EIGHTH SOLDIER: (To the Eighteenth.) Why don't you ask him?

EIGHTEENTH SOLDIER: *(To the body.)* You ever been in Paris, Mac?... *(To the others.)* Anyone know how to say that in German?

(Lieutenant Finley enters the circle.)

FINLEY: Take your last look, men. The Captain wants the area cleared.

EIGHTH SOLDIER: Why?

FINLEY: He doesn't like the idea of you all standing around up here. *(To the Thirteenth Soldier.)* You stay. Tell anyone else who comes that it's off limits.

THIRTEENTH SOLDIER: Yes sir.

FINLEY: *(To the others.)* The rest of you take off.

FIRST SOLDIER: *(As they go off.)* The old man sure gets some funny notions.

FIFTH SOLDIER: Yeah.

EIGHTEENTH SOLDIER: *(To the body.)* See you around, buddy.

(They all go off leaving the Thirteenth Soldier and Lieutenant Finley.)

FINLEY: *(To the Thirteenth Soldier.)* Hope you don't get lonely.

THIRTEENTH SOLDIER: *(Indicating the body.)* We're old friends.

FINLEY: I'll send someone to relieve you. *(He goes off.)*

(Alone, the Thirteenth Soldier looks at the body a moment, then turns away, looks around casually to see if anyone's there, then looks at the body again. Begins to whistle idly. Now Revere appears at the edge of the clearing and halts.)

THIRTEENTH SOLDIER: Hi, Revere.

REVERE: *(Looking at the body.)* Hi.

THIRTEENTH SOLDIER: You can't stay here. The old man's put it off limits.

REVERE: You on guard?

THIRTEENTH SOLDIER: Yeah.

REVERE: *(Hold's up the tags.)* I got his dog tags.

THIRTEENTH SOLDIER: From Webb.

REVERE: Yes. I want to put them back. Okay?

THIRTEENTH SOLDIER: I guess so, but do it quick.

(Revere makes no move.)

THIRTEENTH SOLDIER: What are you waiting for? Go on.

(Revere approaches the body with great reluctance and loathing. Reaching the body, he stands looking down at it.)

THIRTEENTH SOLDIER: Will you please hurry up?

(Revere hesitates a moment more, contemplates flight, then abruptly he stoops down and replaces the dog tags on the body. When he rises from this task his face is white, and pained. He turns away from the body and lowers his head.)

THIRTEENTH SOLDIER: What's the matter?

(Revere doesn't answer.)

THIRTEENTH SOLDIER: You feel all right? *(He comes close to Revere and looks at him.)* You gonna be sick or something?

(Revere now races off. The Thirteenth Soldier looks after him, puzzled. At the Captain's Billet. The Captain and Finley are present. The Exec Officer enters.)

EXEC: Message just in from Division.

(Hands a paper to the Captain who reads it, then rises and goes to the map.)

CAPTAIN: At thirteen hundred we have to be *there.*

(He points to a spot on the map. The others look.)

CAPTAIN: That's about ten kilometers. *(Looks at his watch.)* I have eleven fourteen.

(The Exec and Finley check their watches. The Exec finds his accurate. Finley makes an adjustment.)

CAPTAIN: We'll pull out of here at twelve hundred. *(To the Exec.)* I want to see all the officers.

EXEC: Yes sir. *(He goes out.)*

CAPTAIN: *(To Finley.)* Your platoon gets the first mission. You'll be in action before dark.

FINLEY: Any particulars?

CAPTAIN: Yes, but I'll save them till the rest get here. *(Preoccupied.)* How do you think your bunch will do?

FINLEY: As well as any of the others.

CAPTAIN: Yes, I guess so... *(Now, his back to Finley, he approaches the subject that is on his mind.)* Finley.

FINLEY: Sir?

CAPTAIN: I've changed my mind. After the briefing I want you to see to it that German is buried.

FINLEY: *(Flatly.)* Yes sir.

CAPTAIN: Somehow I feel it's my duty. One of those things that would bother me the rest of my life if I didn't attend to it.

FINLEY: *(Dutifully.)* Yes sir.

CAPTAIN: You don't approve.

FINLEY: No sir.

CAPTAIN: Why not?

FINLEY: *(Ambiguously.)* It'll be tough digging. The ground around here is hard.

(The Exec and three other officers enter and collect around the map where the Captain briefs them while our attention turns to: The Soldiers' Billet. The Sergeant still lies on the floor staring at the ceiling. The Sixth Soldier is

asleep. *The Fourth Soldier is sitting idly. He shoots occasional looks of puzzlement at the Sergeant. At one side of the room the crap game has resumed. Involved are the Third, Fifth, Seventh, Eighth, Eleventh Soldiers and the Medic. The Third Soldier throws the dice.)*

THIRD SOLDIER: Ho dice!

EIGHTH SOLDIER: Four's the point.

(The Third Soldier picks up the dice, shakes them.)

THIRD SOLDIER: *(Blowing on the dice.)* Twenty-two right back. *(He throws a five.)*

ELEVENTH SOLDIER: Down a mile.

THIRD SOLDIER: *(Picking up the dice.)* I'll take the odds.

(No one offers them. Shakes the dice.)

THIRD SOLDIER: You saved money, boys. *(Throws a ten.)* It's on the other side. *(Picks up the dice.)* Still looking for the odds.

(He shakes the dice and is about to throw when Revere enters. They all know where he's been and from his drained, dazed appearance it is plain that it has been a terrible experience for him. Without a word they all turn and watch him as he walks across the room and drops on his sack.)

FOURTH SOLDIER: *(To Revere, solicitously.)* You put them back?

(Revere nods yes.)

FOURTH SOLDIER: You feel all right?

REVERE: Yes.

FOURTH SOLDIER: You sure?

REVERE: *Yes! (He rolls over on his stomach, buries his head and begins to cry muffledly.)*
(The others watch with sympathetic embarrassment.)

FOURTH SOLDIER: *(To Revere.)* Can I get you something?

SEVENTH SOLDIER: *(To the Fourth, with quiet certainty and understanding.)* Let him alone. He'll be all right. *(He motions the Third Soldier to resume the crap game.)*

THIRD SOLDIER: Four's my point, right?

EIGHTH SOLDIER: Yeah.

(The crap shooters return to the game.)

THIRD SOLDIER: *(Without his previous enthusiasm as he shakes the dice.)* Let me see a four. *(He throws.)*

FIFTH SOLDIER: You lose.

(The faders take their money. As they do the Sergeant gets to his feet.)

SERGEANT: *(To the Fourth Soldier.)* Anyone wants me I'm at the clearing.

FOURTH SOLDIER: It's off limits.

(The Sergeant gives no sign he's heard and exits. The Medic takes the dice, puts down money.)

MEDIC: Shoot what's there.

FIFTH SOLDIER: I'll take ten.

THIRD SOLDIER: I'll take the same.

ELEVENTH SOLDIER: What's open?

THIRD SOLDIER: Fifteen.

ELEVENTH SOLDIER: I got it.

(Lieutenant Finley enters.)

FINLEY: *(To the men in the crap game.)* If you'll hold it a minute, I have some news. *(They turn from the game to him. When he has their attention, he speaks.)*

FINLEY: It is my privilege to announce that this is it: We're pulling out in forty minutes. We'll see action before the day's over. I'll fill you in on the details later. Right now I'm looking for four men who crave a little exercise.

EIGHTH SOLDIER: Doing what?

FINLEY: Digging a hole for our friend up in the clearing.

ELEVENTH SOLDIER: You mean bury him?

FINLEY: That's right. Any volunteers?

ELEVENTH SOLDIER: I'll go.

THIRD SOLDIER: *(Angrily.)* Sure you will. You're way ahead.

ELEVENTH SOLDIER: *(To the Third.)* Ah, blow it.

FINLEY: Anyone else?

(No answers.)

FINLEY: Okay then, it'll be you... *(Points to the Third Soldier.)* You... *(Points to the Fifth.)* And Revere.

(He looks at Revere, who gives no sign he's heard.)

FINLEY: *(Continued.)* You hear me, Revere?

(No response.)

FOURTH SOLDIER: *(To the Lieutenant.)* He don't feel good.

FINLEY: What's wrong?

FOURTH SOLDIER: I don't know...I wouldn't mind some exercise, sir.

FINLEY: Okay, you're the fourth. *(To the others.)* The rest of you get ready to move out. *(To the four.)* Let's go.

(He goes. The four follow him. The last man out is the Fourth Soldier. Revere, without turning over, speaks to him before he exits.)

REVERE: Thanks, Watka.

FOURTH SOLDIER: Forget it. *(He exits.)*

EIGHTH SOLDIER: *(Angrily.)* I'd like to get my hands on the guy who started that song and dance about taking prisoners to Paris.

SEVENTH SOLDIER: It kept you happy for a little while. What more do you want from a rumor? *(He shakes the Sixth Soldier.)* Hey...Hey. *(No response.)*

SEVENTH SOLDIER: Hey, wake up.

(The Sixth Soldier, after rough shaking, wakens.)

SIXTH SOLDIER: What's the matter? What's up?

SEVENTH SOLDIER: *(To the Sixth.)* There's a war on.

(At the Clearing, the Sergeant is looking at the body, the Thirteenth Soldier is beside him trying to get him to leave.)

THIRTEENTH SOLDIER: I'm not supposed to let anybody up here, Sarge. *(No response.)*

THIRTEENTH SOLDIER: It's the Captain's orders. Finley spots you, I'll get my ass in a sling.

(The Sergeant stares at the corpse, giving no indication that he's heard.)

THIRTEENTH SOLDIER: Hey, Sarge, be a sport...Sarge.

(The Sergeant goes on staring and now the Thirteenth Soldier becomes interested. He looks down at the body trying to see what it is that so engrosses the Sergeant.)

THIRTEENTH SOLDIER: What is it?...What do you see?

SERGEANT: *(Without looking away from the body.)* What do *you* see?

THIRTEENTH SOLDIER: *(Puzzled.)* A dead German.

SERGEANT: What else?

THIRTEENTH SOLDIER: What else is there?

SERGEANT: *(With quiet certainty.)* You see just like the rest. But no one wants to say it.

THIRTEENTH SOLDIER: Say what?

(The Sergeant doesn't answer.)

THIRTEENTH SOLDIER: I don't follow you.

SERGEANT: *(Matter-of-factly, sadly.)* He looks like me.

(The Thirteenth Soldier looks at the corpse.)

THIRTEENTH SOLDIER: Gee, I don't see that.

SERGEANT: *(Looks at the Thirteenth Soldier.)* Why do you all lie? What's it matter if he looks like me?

THIRTEENTH SOLDIER: *(Now afraid, seeks to appease.)* Yeah. Yeah. I guess so.

(The Lieutenant and the grave diggers approach the clearing.)

THIRTEENTH SOLDIER: Sarge, somebody's coming. Would you go? Please?

SERGEANT: Okay. *(He exits from the clearing.)*

(The Lieutenant, carrying a hammer, enters the clearing with the Third, Fourth, Fifth and Eleventh Soldiers. The latter two have shovels.)

FINLEY: *(To the Thirteenth.)* You can take off.

THIRTEENTH SOLDIER: Yes sir. *(Then, curious at their paraphernalia.)* What are you going to do?

FINLEY: Bury him.

THIRTEENTH SOLDIER: Why?

THIRD SOLDIER: *(Sarcastically.)* He's dead.

> *(The Fifth and Fourth Soldiers laugh. The Thirteenth goes off. The Lieutenant looks around and then selects a spot on the side of the clearing.)*

FINLEY: I guess this is as good as any place. *(To the Fifth and Eleventh.)* You two start in.

ELEVENTH SOLDIER: *(As he and the Fifth are about to dig.)* How deep you want it?

FINLEY: You dig. I'll tell you when to stop.

FIFTH SOLDIER: *(As he digs.)* I don't see why *we* have to bury him. It'd be different if we were the ones who killed him.

ELEVENTH SOLDIER: Yeah.

THIRD SOLDIER: In my opinion, the whole idea stems from the fact that the old man has a neatness complex.

FINLEY: *(To the Third.)* Anyone ask for your opinion? *(To the diggers.)* Make it snappy. There isn't much time.

FOURTH SOLDIER: What sort of a deal we in for this afternoon, Lieutenant?

FINLEY: We're going to try and capture a bridge before it's blown up.

FIFTH SOLDIER: *(As he digs.)* How come we got the first mission?

FINLEY: I guess it's because we're the first platoon.

eleventh soldier: Why didn't we draw for it or something?

THIRD SOLDIER: Because it's not a draw bridge.

ELEVENTH SOLDIER: *(Heatedly to the Third.)* Why don't you can your crap a while?

THIRD SOLDIER: *(To the Eleventh.)* I'm sorry. I didn't realize you were so edgy.

FINLEY: *(To the diggers.)* Okay, change over.

> *(The Fifth and Eleventh Soldiers hand their shovels to the Third and Fourth who begin to dig. The Lieutenant speaks to the Eleventh Soldier.)*

FINLEY: Check his pockets for personal effects and get one of his dog tags to put on the marker.

> *(The Eleventh moves to do so. The Lieutenant turns to the Fifth and hands him the hammer and some nails.)*

FINLEY: Take this and make a cross out of something.

> *(Captain's Billet. The Captain is at the map. The Exec comes in.)*

CAPTAIN: Everything under control?

EXEC: Yes sir.

CAPTAIN: Finley is burying that German.

EXEC: I know.

CAPTAIN: It's a great load off my mind. *(Indicating the checker board.)* How about a game or two?

EXEC: All right.

CAPTAIN: It might be a while before we play again.

(They set up the pieces. The Soldiers' Billet. Present are the First, Second, Sixth, Seventh Soldiers, Revere and the Sergeant. The Sergeant is packing his gear. The Sixth, his gear packed, is sitting trying to fight off a hangover. The Seventh Soldier, his gear packed, is lying against it, his eyes closed, but not sleeping. The Second Soldier, his gear packed, is trying to wrap his bayonet souvenir for mailing home. He is doing a sloppy job. The First Soldier sits beside him watching.)

SECOND SOLDIER: *(Holding up the finished product doubtfully.)* You think it'll get through the mails like this?

FIRST SOLDIER: No.

(Second Soldier unwraps the bayonet and begins to rewrap it. At the Clearing:)

FINLEY: *(To the Third and Fourth Soldiers, who are digging.)* Just a little more.

FOURTH SOLDIER: It won't be any six feet.

FINLEY: I don't care.

(The Captain's Billet.)

CAPTAIN: *(To the Exec as they play.)* What I mean is we don't have to behave like a bunch of savages because we're at war.

EXEC: I agree. *(Makes a double jump, winning a game.)* That puts me fifteen up. *(They set up the pieces. The Soldiers' Billet. Webb comes in carrying a German helmet. He displays it to the Second Soldier triumphantly.)*

WEBB: There, take a look at that. That's what I call a souvenir.

SECOND SOLDIER: *(Enviously.)* Where'd you get it?

WEBB: In that ditch by the road we came in on.

SECOND SOLDIER: I looked there.

WEBB: But you didn't look hard enough.

SEVENTH SOLDIER: *(Without opening his eyes.)* You boys keep snooping and one of these days you'll run into a booby trap. *(That touches off an idea and he sits up.)* Did anyone check that body up there for a booby trap?

SIXTH SOLDIER: *(Wearily indicating the First and Second Soldiers.)* Our two Rover Boys turned him over looking for souvenirs.

SECOND SOLDIER: No, we didn't.

SIXTH SOLDIER: *(Indicating the First Soldier.)* He said you did.

SECOND SOLDIER: No.

(They look at him.)

SECOND SOLDIER: We didn't. *(Turns to the First Soldier.)* Why did you say that?

FIRST SOLDIER: I thought there might be something underneath him and we could look later when the rest went away.

(At the Clearing. The Fourth and Third stand by the hole leaning on their shovels. The Fifth stands next to them holding the cross he's made. They watch the Lieutenant and the Eleventh Soldier, who bend to pick up the corpse. At the Soldiers' Billet:)

SEVENTH SOLDIER: I think somebody better go up there and—

(There is an explosion at the clearing as the body is lifted. The Lieutenant and the Eleventh Soldier topple. The Fourth falls to his knees, the Third holds his shoulder, the Fifth, shielded by the Third and Fourth, just gapes dumbstruck with horror. In the Billet they look at each other, exchanging the horrible thought. At the Captain's Billet.)

CAPTAIN: *(Listening.)* What was that? *What do you suppose that was?*

(At the Clearing, the Fourth Soldier whimpers softly.)

THIRD SOLDIER: *(Distantly, trance-like.)* My arm, I think. Could you attend to my arm. Could someone attend to my arm. Could you…My arm…I think…My arm…My arm.

(Now the Fifth Soldier erupts, drops the cross and runs in terror from the Clearing.)

FIFTH SOLDIER: *(Screaming.)* Help! Help! Help!

THE END

THE GOLF BALL

INTRODUCTION

If I were forced to retire from writing and had sufficient funds to entertain myself in any way I desired, it wouldn't be sufficient.

For many (most?) retired men, fun, games, hobbies, volunteer work, grandchildren, and friends fill the bill.

I know that because I occasionally visit a boyhood friend (the happiest retiree I know) at Hilton Head.

He and his friends radiate contentment.

But somewhere on that idyllic isle must be a man who chafes.

Of such exceptions is drama born.

My wife says if I retired no one would know the difference.

I'm afraid to ask her what she means.

ORIGINAL PRODUCTION

The Golf Ball was presented at the Ensemble Studio Theatre Marathon in 1999. The play was directed by Chris Smith, sets by Kenichi Toki, costumes by Amela Baksic, lighting by Greg Macpherson, with the following cast:

Charlie . . . . Baxter Harris
Agnes . . . . Mimi Bensinger
George . . . . Tom Ligon

PRODUCTION NOTE

Chris Smith, the director, devised a contraption that allowed the golf ball to be teed up (Scene VI), whacked for all it was worth, and magically disappear.

The effect was mesmerizing.

Unfortunately it was devised too late to perfect. Fearing malfunction and injuring a member of the audience we jettisoned the notion and went with pantomime.

For those who never saw the ball struck and vanish, it worked. But having seen the real thing I felt deprived.

Should you want to duplicate that striking effect, I recommend you get a good machinist and a good lawyer just in case.

SCENE I

Time: Morning—the present. Place: the Powell's kitchen. At rise: George and Agnes Powell, late fifties, at breakfast. She, in housecoat, reading a newspaper. He, dressed for golf—his clubs visible.

AGNES: *(Head buried in the paper.)* …What time do you tee off?

GEORGE: Same as always.

AGNES: Charlie's late.

GEORGE: Hopefully he's overslept, had a flat, won't come at all.
(This occasions a look from her.)

AGNES: …Here's one for you: A wealthy retired CEO held up a gas station—
(He snatches the paper from her.)

AGNES: Pardon *me.*

GEORGE: *(Finds the story.)* "Captured by police after a high speed chase, Mr. A. E. Gantley, former head of Hawking Industries said, 'It's the most fun I've had in years.'"

AGNES: Sounds drunk or senile.

GEORGE: *(Reading.)* "Mr. Gantley passed a sobriety test and has no history of mental illness."

AGNES: Why did he do it then?

GEORGE: Maybe he couldn't face another round of golf.

AGNES: Here we go again.

GEORGE: *(Reading.)* "What the gas station attendant took for a gun proved to be Mr. Gantley's eyeglass case."

AGNES: He's lucky he wasn't killed.

GEORGE: Or unlucky depending on his objective.

AGNES: Not funny.

GEORGE: Not meant to be.

AGNES: We're healthy. Our children and grandchildren are fine. We have friends—money. What more do you want?

GEORGE: Mrs. Gantley's exact words to Mr. Gantley as he pulled into the gas station intending to say "Fill it up" and said "Stick 'em up" instead.
(Agnes grabs the paper—scans.)

AGNES: Where does it say that?

GEORGE: I was kidding.
(A car horn sounds.)

AGNES: Charlie's here.

GEORGE: Alas.

AGNES: If you're tired of golf, play tennis; take a bike ride, go swimming.

GEORGE: You left out shuffleboard and nature walk.

AGNES: Better yet write a book on the dangers of early retirement.

GEORGE: Low blow.

AGNES: Apologies. For what it's worth, I love you.

GEORGE: I love you too.

(The car horn again impatiently. He kisses her on the cheek; gets his golf clubs.)

AGNES: Promise you won't rob a gas station?

GEORGE: You have my word. *(He exits.)*

SCENE II

At rise: A moving car, Charlie Olsen, late fifties, driving. George beside him.

CHARLIE: I think I found the secret.

(No reaction from George.)

CHARLIE: Don't you want to know what it is?

GEORGE: More than life.

CHARLIE: Concentrate on one thing at a time. Today it's going to be, 'Take the club back slowly.' S-L-O-W-L-Y. Everything else: hip turn, weight distribution, grip, follow through—I'm putting out of my mind.

GEORGE: You're driving too fast.

CHARLIE: We're late. We lose our tee-off time we might not get another.

GEORGE: We should be so lucky.

CHARLIE: Lucky?

GEORGE: If we can't play golf we'll do something else.

CHARLIE: My knee rules out tennis and it's too late to go fishing.

GEORGE: I was thinking of something different.

CHARLIE: Such as?

GEORGE: There's a bank up ahead. What do you say we slip the teller a note saying, "Give me all your cash?"

CHARLIE: I'd rather play golf.

GEORGE: Robbing a gas station would be easier but I promised Agnes I wouldn't.

CHARLIE: *(He's got it now.)* The guy in the paper this morning—Gantley.

GEORGE: Right.

CHARLIE: He's got to be nuts.

GEORGE: I'm not sure.

CHARLIE: *(Turning to him.)* A retired CEO robbing a gas station isn't crazy?

GEORGE: Keep your eyes on the road.

SCENE III

Place: The first tee. At rise: Charlie practice swinging. George standing by.

CHARLIE: *(Bringing the club back in slow motion.)* S-L-O-W-L-Y. Usual stakes?

GEORGE: No. Let's make it interesting.

CHARLIE: How much?

GEORGE: Everything I own against everything you own.

CHARLIE: How about twenty a side plus lunch?

GEORGE: I said 'interesting'

CHARLIE: You name it.

GEORGE: I did.

CHARLIE: *(Going with what he assumes to be a gag.)* All I have against all you have?

GEORGE: Right.

CHARLIE: Including Swiss bank accounts?

GEORGE: Everything. What do you say?

CHARLIE: It's not fair.

GEORGE: Why?

CHARLIE: I think I have more than you.

GEORGE: I'm worth seven million. What about you?

CHARLIE: *(A hint of uneasiness.)* What about me?

GEORGE: How much money do you have?

CHARLIE: *(Trying to make light of it.)* I refuse to answer on the grounds—

GEORGE: —You told me about your mistress—your prostate problems. You won't tell me how much money you have.

CHARLIE: What's the punch line?

GEORGE: Punch line implies joke. I'm serious.

CHARLIE: *(Looking off.)* The starter's waving. We better get going.
(George reaches into his bag for a ball.)

GEORGE: *Damn.*

CHARLIE: What is it?

GEORGE: I was chipping balls on my lawn—forgot to pack them.

CHARLIE: No balls?

GEORGE: *(Holding up a ball.)* Except this one.

CHARLIE: You better go and get some.

GEORGE: You don't think I can play eighteen holes with one ball?

CHARLIE: I know so and I only have a few myself.

GEORGE: How much you want to bet?

CHARLIE: You've never played eighteen holes without losing two or three balls at least.

GEORGE: How much?

CHARLIE: I'd be stealing your money.

GEORGE: Put up or shut up.

CHARLIE: *(Irritated.) Five hundred bucks.*

GEORGE: You're on. *(Regarding the ball.)* It's a Titleist One. *(Hands the ball to Charlie.)* Write your initials on it.

CHARLIE: I trust you.

GEORGE: I insist.

CHARLIE: You're not serious about this?

GEORGE: Trying to weasel out of it?

(Charlie initials the ball; hands it to George.)

CHARLIE: Your honor.

(George tees up; prepares to hit.)

SCENE IV

Place: In the rough. At rise: George looking for his ball. Charlie standing by.

CHARLIE: How much longer?

GEORGE: Till I find it.

CHARLIE: There's a foursome breathing down our necks.

GEORGE: Wave them through.

CHARLIE: At this rate we'll be all day.

GEORGE: You're in a hurry, go. I'll catch up.

CHARLIE: You've been looking for fifteen minutes.

GEORGE: Is there a time limit?

CHARLIE: The bet's off. I'll give you another ball.

GEORGE: *The bet's on.*

CHARLIE: *(Glancing back.)* That foursome's teeing off. I'm going, George.

GEORGE: See you later.

(Charlie goes off. George resumes the search.)

SCENE V

Place: The clubhouse. At rise: Charlie at lunch. George appears.

CHARLIE: Look who's here…Well?

GEORGE: Guess.

CHARLIE: You couldn't find it.

GEORGE: Guess again.

CHARLIE: You found it but then you lost it again.

GEORGE: Right.

CHARLIE: Make the check out to cash.

GEORGE: I lost it and found it three times. *(Displaying the ball.)* Note the letters "C.H." in your own inimitable hand.

CHARLIE: *(Inspecting the ball.)* You played all nine holes?

GEORGE: Shot a fifty-three—my best score ever.

CHARLIE: You've still got nine to go and the back side's a lot tougher.

GEORGE: Care to make it a thousand?

CHARLIE: What about the sixteenth?

GEORGE: What about it?

CHARLIE: You usually drop your ball on the other side of the pond and take a penalty.

GEORGE: No drop today.

CHARLIE: You're going to try and hit across?

GEORGE: I *am* going to hit across.

CHARLIE: You've never cleared the water in all the times we played.

GEORGE: A thousand too rich for your blood?

CHARLIE: *A thousand it is!*

SCENE VI

Place: The sixteenth tee. At rise: George and Charlie arrive.

GEORGE: *(Displaying the ball.)* Fifteen down and three holes to go. Getting nervous?

CHARLIE: Don't look now but that water staring you in the face is two hundred yards across.

GEORGE: *(To the ball.)* Is he trying to rattle us?

CHARLIE: Use the ladies' tee. Give yourself a chance at least.

GEORGE: No thanks. My honor?

CHARLIE: Right.

GEORGE: Last chance to increase your wager.

CHARLIE: I feel guilty enough as it is.

GEORGE: *(To the ball.)* Till we meet again.

CHARLIE: What you mean is goodbye forever.

(George tees up, takes several practice swings. Pauses...Focuses... Concentrates... Hits.)

CHARLIE: *(Impressed.)* Wow.

(Both men follow the ball's flight.)

GEORGE: What do you think?

CHARLIE: Best drive you ever hit.

GEORGE: It's got a chance.

CHARLIE: It's going to be close.

GEORGE: *Get up there—get up there!*

(Both men follow the balls trajectory to a watery finish.)

GEORGE: Splash.

CHARLIE: No cigar but one helluva try.

GEORGE: Five yards short?

CHARLIE: Give or take.

GEORGE: *(Marking where the ball landed.)* On a line with that willow tree and the flag stick?

CHARLIE: What difference does it make?

GEORGE: Lucky it's summer.

CHARLIE: Why?

GEORGE: The water will be warm.

CHARLIE: You're not thinking...

GEORGE: If the fat lady sang, I missed it.

SCENE VII

Place: Beside the pond. At rise: George removing shoes, socks and rolling up his pants. Charlie incredulous.

CHARLIE: There are snakes in there. Snapping turtles. God knows what.

GEORGE: I haven't done this since I was a kid.

CHARLIE: What are people going to think?

GEORGE: Frankly, I don't give a fuck.

CHARLIE: You're beginning to worry me.

GEORGE: *(Pants rolled—sighting.)* Flagstick—willow—tee. Line them up like so and the ball should be right about there. *(Pointing.)* What do you think?

CHARLIE: I'm leaving, George.

GEORGE: Would you mind calling Agnes and tell her I'll be late?

SCENE VIII

Place: The Powell's kitchen. At rise: Agnes lost in thought. George, bearing his golf clubs, enters.

AGNES: At last.

GEORGE: Didn't Charlie tell you I'd be late?

AGNES: Yes.

(The phone beside her rings. She ignores it.)

GEORGE: Aren't you going to answer it?

AGNES: It'll be someone asking if you're all right. I've had a dozen calls like that so far.

GEORGE: I'm fine. Why wouldn't I be?

AGNES: A prominent citizen with his pants rolled trying to find a golf ball in a filthy pond makes people wonder.

GEORGE: What did you tell them?

AGNES: Observe. *(She picks up the ringing phone.)* Hello?…Hi Madge… Correct…Pants rolled—wading…Because Charlie bet him he couldn't play eighteen holes without losing a ball…I hope you're right… Bye. *(She hangs up.)*

GEORGE: You hope she's right about what?

AGNES: She said, "Boys will be boys."

GEORGE: A dozen calls?

AGNES: At least. You frightened Charlie.

GEORGE: He scares easy.

AGNES: You frightened me and I don't scare easy.

GEORGE: What's for supper—I'm famished.

AGNES: Charlie said you should give it to the Red Cross.

GEORGE: It?

AGNES: The thousand dollars.

GEORGE: He hasn't won yet.

AGNES: Does that mean you're going to keep looking for the ball?

GEORGE: I don't have to look for it. *(Revealing the ball.) Voila.*

AGNES: You found it?

GEORGE: Just as the sun set.

AGNES: It's over then.

GEORGE: Almost.

AGNES: Almost?

GEORGE: I've got two holes to go.

AGNES: I'm sure Charlie will concede.

GEORGE: That's not the point.

AGNES: What *is* the point, George?

GEORGE: I have to play the last two holes.

AGNES: Hook your tee shot on the eighteenth you're back in the pond again.

GEORGE: I'll slice deliberately.

AGNES: Suppose the ball hits a sprinkler or the cart path and bounces into the water?

GEORGE: The odds against that are incalculable.

AGNES: One of the calls was from the club president quoting the rule that forbids members from entering water hazards.

GEORGE: This ball will not end up in the water.

AGNES: But if by some miracle it does, will you admit defeat?

GEORGE: I can't.

AGNES: You'll roll up your pants and wade in?

GEORGE: Yes.

AGNES: For how long?

GEORGE: Until I find it.

AGNES: We'll be kicked out of the club, ridiculed, lose our friends.

GEORGE: Would that be the end of the world?

AGNES: It would be the end of *my* world. Not the world I fancied as a child but the world I'm stuck with and intend to make the best of.

GEORGE: Stuck with?

AGNES: *Stuck with.* Don't you think *Mrs.* Gantley ever felt like robbing a gas station?

GEORGE: It's different for men.

AGNES: Right. *You* pick the dream. *We* tag along. If it doesn't end up the way we hoped, we grin and bear it.

GEORGE: You knew what my goals were before we married.

AGNES: True.

GEORGE: You encouraged and supported them.

AGNES: Also true.

GEORGE: Did I accomplish everything I said I would?

AGNES: Yes. And there's the rub.

GEORGE: What do you mean?

AGNES: You dreamed too small.

GEORGE: You never complained before.

AGNES: You never waded in a scummy pond looking for a golf ball before.

GEORGE: You win: I won't play the last two holes.

AGNES: I'm afraid you have to.

GEORGE: Why?

AGNES: If you don't we'd always wonder what difference it might have made.

GEORGE: Suppose by some fluke the ball goes in the water?

AGNES: And you look for it?

GEORGE: Yes.

AGNES: When you come home I'll be gone.

GEORGE: Why?

AGNES: I don't believe in flukes.

GEORGE: Where will you go?

AGNES: First to visit Mrs. Gantley. After that who knows.

GEORGE: I'm going out early in the morning. Two holes—I'll be back in time for breakfast.

AGNES: I hope so George. *(Touching his cheek lovingly.)* I really do.

GEORGE: It'll be a breeze thanks to a tip from Charlie. He said forget about everything except taking the club back slowly. *(He takes a driver from his bag. Sets the golf ball on the floor. His back to her, he demonstrates.)* S-L-O-W-L-Y.

(As he spells and takes the club back, Agnes exits.)

GEORGE: What do you think?

(When she doesn't respond, he turns—finds her gone.)

GEORGE: Agnes?…Agnes?…

(Lights narrow on the golf ball.)

THE END

Frank D. Gilroy is a playwright, novelist, television writer, screen writer, director, and independent filmmaker. His awards include a Pulitzer Prize, a Tony Award and A Drama Critics Award for *The Subject Was Roses.* His play *Who'll Save the Plowboy?* won the Obie for Best American Play of the Year. *Desperate Characters,* which he wrote and directed, won two Silver Bears at the Berlin Film Festival. Born and raised in the Bronx, he graduated from Dartmouth (courtesy of the GI Bill) after service in World War II. He is a past president of the Dramatists Guild.